The 50⁺ Best Books on TEXAS

The 50+
Best Books
on
T·E·X·A·S

by
A. C. Greene

University of North Texas Press

Denton, Texas

Requests for permission to reproduce materials from this book should
be directed to:

Permissions
University of North Texas Press
PO Box 311336
Denton TX 76203-1336
phone 940-565-2142
fax 940-565-4590

The paper used in this book meets the minimum requirements
of the American National Standard for Permanence of Paper
for Printed Library Materials, z39.48.1984. Binding materials
have been chosen for durability.

Library of Congress Cataloging-in-Publication Data

Greene, A. C., 1923–
The 50 plus best books on Texas / A. C. Greene.
p.   cm.
Updated ed. of: The 50 best books on Texas. 1982.
Includes index.
ISBN 1-57441-043-1 (alk. paper)
1. Texas—Bibliography. 2. Best books—Texas. I. Greene A. C.,
1923–   Fifty best books on Texas. II. Title.
Z1339.G73   1998
[F386]   97-49625
016.9764—dc21   CIP

Design by Accent Design and Communications

This one's for Angus Cameron, editor, mentor, but mostly, friend. He put me on the path I'm still climbing.

Contents

Introduction to the Original Edition

These are, my choice, the fifty best books about Texas—and I'd like to emphasize, they are my choice because I like them. I would also like to emphasize that these are the best books about Texas. By that I mean, Texas is their main subject or, in the case of fiction and biography, their chief setting. They are not the best books written by Texas authors (in fact, not all the authors are Texans) and they may not be the most important Texas books—but don't let's get off into a thicket of objectives and explanations: the quality of the books speaks for itself. I think they are the best.

When this idea was first proposed, it was suggested that a list of the best hundred Texas books be made, but I said no. While a hundred good titles could be assembled, one hundred opens the gate too widely. So, fifty it is.

I have not used any particularly stringent criterion for including a book save the rather inexact one of "good." And, incidentally, the books are not listed in sequence of preference or ranked in any other way. I have not attempted to pick something from each form of literature, but I haven't slighted any type of writing, either, unless you might say I excluded textbooks and technical manuals. But, frankly, if I had been attracted to a book of that sort, I would not have hesitated to include it.

I am not guilty of picking books written by friends. True, I know and like (or knew and liked) several of the authors whose works I have chosen, but as you will discover if you read the notes on the individual titles, I have not been universally liked by those whose books I have chosen. Knowing the author shouldn't make a book better, or worse, in one's critical judgment.

There are a number of fine Texas writers not represented on my list of fifty best books. In virtually every case it is because they have not written books about Texas. That certainly explains the absence of a title by Frances Mossiker or Leon Harris (although Leon came close with his famous adaptation, "The Night Before Christmas; In Texas, That Is"). Donald Barthelme, a notable Texan of letters, while a genius, did only a few short stories involving his Texas antecedents. Marshall Terry, a Texan most of his life, wrote a small masterpiece, *Tom Northway*, but old Tom lived his ninety years in Ohio.

There are certain books one might think would appear automatically on a list of Texas best, for example, *The Devil Rides Outside* by the late Texas writer John Howard Griffin; but again it's not about Texas. Bill Goetzmann's *Exploration and Empire* won the Pulitzer history prize, among others, and established a new way of writing western history, but, alas, has less than a tiny portion on Texas. Edward Weems's *To Conquer a Peace* is one of the most readable things done on the Mexican War, but once more, Texas is a minor part of its history.

The fifty best of Texas will change through the years—my own choices will change if I live a few more years, I am sure. Some titles may make other lists in later days: Elmer Kelton's *The Time It Never Rained* and Stephen Harrigan's *Aransas* I feel pretty sure of; Andrew Jolly's *A Time of Soldiers*, and Gary Cartwright's *Blood Will Tell*, could easily score, and so might Harry Hurt III's *Texas Rich: The Hunt Dynasty*.

There was one book I planned to include until I read the author's introduction (to the Time Reading Program edition). That was *The Sea of Grass*, by Conrad Richter. Even Frank Dobie thought it was a Texas book when he first read it (according to Richter), but the author specifically denies the Texas taint.

Someone may ask, what about Edna Ferber's *Giant?* I happen to think *Giant* is a bad book; a spiteful piece, crippled by the author's regional ignorance and her inability to separate Hollywood caricature from Texas character. Any other questions? Well, there's *The Wind* by Dorothy Scarborough. *The Wind* is a ridiculous novel telling how those bad ol' West Texas elements drove mad a gentle Virginia blueblood cast out on the frontier. Perhaps she had a right to go mad, being powerless to leave the narrative and escape the author's non-stop, three-year (honest to God!) sand storm. Come to think of it, both heroines—of *Giant* and of *The Wind*—were Virginian FFVs. Maybe Virginia ladies should stay out of Texas fiction?

There are other books I wish I could stick in regardless of scant Texas references, just because so few people know they have any Texas references at all; books like Thornton Wilder's

Heaven's My Destination and Arthur Lewis's *The Day They Shook the Plum Tree,* delightful reading. Then, there are books such as *The Death of a President* by William Manchester, the best known of the Kennedy assassination books, or the Warren Commission report itself; wherever they might belong, I have left them out.

I have not included any sets, although one could argue that Carlos Casteñada's *Our Catholic Heritage* in seven volumes is as good as any historical work done on Texas. But one has to draw a line. I have not included any of the Cabeza de Vaca narratives, or reports from early Spanish expeditions. For that matter, I've shied away from almost all history-as-history books. Many are quite valuable, but this is not the 50 most *valuable* books about Texas.

There are some titles missing which are standard titles in "Texas Best." Most are cowboy and cattle industry books, such as *We Pointed Them North, Riata and Spur, Log of a Cowboy, Trail Drivers of Texas,* or *The Cowboy and His Interpreters.* They are excellent research sources (I've used them all), but, again a personal observation, I think Texas has moved out of the part of its historic past which includes so many range and cattle books. They once represented a considerable segment of interest of a considerable segment of Texas population. Not anymore. The same thing is true of frontier folklore; it's fading, as are most of the books it produced. In fact, I've never been much on folklore—it has a perverse way of jumping from one region to another by merely changing local names.

In the matter of editions—with most books I have listed the first edition; more as a matter of historical interest than anything else. In a few I have gone to other editions because first editions are untouchable or subsequent editions are better. I have not chosen any book because of its rarity. Several of the books I have picked as "50 best" are available in softcover, and if that suits your taste, feel free; I am not a hardcover snob, although I prefer them. On the other hand, I have not let scarcity stop me from listing a title. A few may be hard to locate, even in Texas libraries—I might say, particularly in Texas libraries; some Texas libraries, like some Texas universities, are fearful of a "regional" tag stuck on them.

Some may ask, why Texas books? Is Texas afraid to stack its art against the general literary art of the nation? Well, Texas is certainly big enough to have its own art; it's larger than a good many important nations. And Texas is one of the few states of the United States that retains a separate identity—for reasons historical, cultural, and political. Part southern, part southwestern, it is neither when it comes to writing about itself. Jump over the border to Louisiana or New Mexico—or even to Oklahoma—and you run into a completely different kind of writing and storytelling . . . different in style, in implications, in what it is striving for.

But I wouldn't for one moment stand up and declare Texas writing greater than the differences. Unfortunately, Texas has not furnished indigenous materials for great novels like LaFarge's *Laughing Boy*, Frank Waters's *The Man Who Killed the Deer*, or Bandelier's *Delight Makers*, as did New Mexico. It has drawn out no *Death Comes for the Archbishop*.

Texas writing, generally, lacks subtlety. Texas is not a subtle place; its societies have not been subtle. Direct, open, candid—the stuff of legend, but not necessarily of literature. Texas writers have been better at telling what was done than what was thought—or what was felt. To know what a Texan did has, most often, been to know what he thought. Texas has always enjoyed asking lots of questions of itself, but it has always gone to the mirror for its answers. Texas takes great delight in studying its reflection in the mirror—even the funhouse mirror. A Texan feels he always has something to fall back on, being Texan, if the questions get uncomfortable.

How long will this list of "Fifty Best" hold up? I can't guess. There are two significant developments which will change literary values in Texas, including mine. First, Texas has attracted a whole tribe of new writers, some already established in American letters, some returning home, and some compelled to try and create artistic emotions to match their cultural excitement—Texas song writers and playwrights have succeeded along this latter line. And the black writers of Texas will have more and more to say about their Texas, past and present—this applies also, of course, to the Hispanic or the Native American writers, making books, stories, poems, plays which may surpass in quality a number of works I include here. Texas is changing rapidly its ways and its tastes. The urbanization of Texas is the next great chapter in Lone Star literature.

And finally, I hope I have not sounded too arbitrary with bold assertions: ". . . this is my pick . . . my choice is . . . this is the best." But I feel there hasn't been enough of this in Texas letters. I think Texas has needed some positive criticism, more outspokenness from within, as regards its own culture. The bold international braggart, when it comes to material trivia, Texas has an inferiority complex about its art.

Behind that mask of bigness, Texas can't believe there is the ability to bring forth, in and of itself, art worthy of mankind's recognition. Texas has relied too long and too completely on the opinions of others.

Do I have the qualifications to make this kind of listing and these comments? Well, as for the first point, I've read everything I endorse, and much of what I have left unnoted. And for what it's worth, I have lived in Texas most of my born'd days and have been intimately associated with Texas writing, books, and authors—not to mention critics, editors, and publishers—for several decades.

But, lacking anything else, I boldly submit my choice for Texas's fifty best books. And, outraged or in agreement, give you leave to make your own.

A. C. Greene
Dallas, 1981

Introduction to the New Edition

In the fifteen years that *The 50 Best Books on Texas* has been around it has become a kind of guidebook to Texas literature, which embarrasses me. *50 Best* has been used by numerous book dealers in their catalogues because I have named several Texas books that no other list maker has included. *50 Best* was not conceived as that, and, as is emphasized in that earlier book, the listings were *my* picks, but not an attempt at converting anyone to my point of view. (The late Johnny Jenkins liked the work, but called it "eccentric.")

This new work, *The 50+ Best Books on Texas*, is, I hope, more than a successor to *The 50 Best Books on Texas*. I offer it as an expanded view—my personal view—of Texas literature up to now. I have included many of the books from that earlier book, but in all but a few entries I have either updated the reports or have added more recent information about the book or the writer, or both. Because I have included title pages for all the books this time (mainly, but not exclusively, for the first edition printing of each), I have left publication information off the heading for each book.

There were writers who didn't like my original choices—the late Frank Tolbert wouldn't speak to me for a few months because I had left out *A Bowl of Red*, but we patched things up long before his death in 1984. The late Donald Barthelme, the most stylistic Texas writer I know of, said to me, (laughingly), "Well, I guess I'm not good enough for you." I tried to explain he had done little Texas-based writing. Larry McMurtry, in his famous essay about Texas writing and writers, "Ever a Bridegroom," called my selections of his work (*Horseman, Pass By* and *Leaving Cheyenne*), "juvenilia" and said I was too good a critic to have included them. I have eliminated *Leaving Cheyenne*, not because it is *juvenilia* but in order to include *Lonesome Dove. Horseman, Pass By*, McMurtry's first book, I think remains the best thing done on the changing social order and commercial realm of modern Texas ranching. At the time of his criticism of my *50 Best* list when it appeared in *Texas Monthly* magazine (the book had not been published), Larry also declared Texas writers should pay more attention to urban Texas, and stop returning to the frontier—then came the publication of *Lonesome Dove*. Larry, while a truly great writer, is given to such pronouncements. In 1986 he told an audience a writer couldn't do good work after age fifty, which age he was approaching. In 1997 he declared he was bored with the American nineteenth century. Disagree with him we may, but he has earned the right to say what he thinks about writing.

Some books of 1983's *50 Best* have been dropped from 1998's *50+ Best. Triggernometry*, for example, while still great reading, seems to be dated in its appeal. I reluctantly removed Katherine Anne Porter's *Pale Horse, Pale Rider* after having to admit it is not specifically a Texas book. *Texas History Movies* has been dropped, not because it might be politically incorrect but because its influence and familiarity have not survived. I read and reread Mary Karr's *The Liar's Club* with an eye to listing it, but while a wonderful study of a tangled Texas family, it does not put much narrative emphasis on its Texas background other than insinuating the natural and climatological sins of the Port Arthur area. Cormac McCarty's *All the Pretty Horses* is a strong, powerful story, but while it skips across the Texas-Mexico border, it is basically a novel of Mexico. Dagoberto Gilb's short stories, like Cormac McCarthy's novels, are strong and powerful, but to date he has been concerned more with social and cultural situations of many places rather than with Texas as a narrative theater. I also pondered Robert Caro's *The Path to Power: The Years of LBJ*, which contains some interesting Hill Country social and historical background, but the viciousness of the second volume seems to cheapen the purpose of the set. Texas, while it has good black poets, lacks black novelists who use Texas as a major influence. Mexican Texans, such as Rolando Hinojosa-Smith and the late Tomás Rivera, have done significant Texas fiction, mainly in Spanish, but translation into English, it appears to me, robs the work of a certain piquancy the Spanish original seems to have expressed.

Texas writing is changing. Perhaps the day will come when there will be no authority, other than historical, for lists such as this of "my favorite" books about Texas. But while the American novel becomes more personal and interior, and national publishing turns more and more to celebrities, certain stories will continue to draw their inspiration and interpretation from the land and culture that surrounds them, and the power of Texas literature will continue to come from that enormous source.

A. C. Greene
Salado, 1998

Adventures with a Texas Naturalist

by Roy Bedichek

Roy Bedichek did not consider himself a philosopher or a historian, but in *Adventures with a Texas Naturalist* he works quite a bit of both assets into his book. And it has continued to work well, beguiling and informing three generations about their inheritance from the Texas lands. The book is as fresh today as it might have been if you had accompanied Bedichek on the travels around the state he describes. Bedichek eventually wrote other books, but *Adventures with a Texas Naturalist* remains his masterwork.

He was older than they were, but for years was held to be a sort of creation of Frank Dobie and Walter Prescott Webb, when all three were sharing company in Austin—the Texas Triumvirate, they have been called. In fact, a statue of the trio was placed in Austin's Zilker Park in the 1990s, to commemorate their close association. Dobie and Webb persuaded Bedichek to isolate himself and write *Adventures with a Texas Naturalist,* and he spent a winter in an upper room at Webb's Friday Mountain Ranch to do so. The results were worth the trouble. Bedichek is an ancient Roman on some pages, a charming philosopher on all pages, and combines enough of the Texas storyteller to suit the reader who doesn't care a hoot about the *havardi* oak or Baruch Spinoza's observations on God and nature.

He wanders off into unbelievable fields of thought no matter which Texas natural wonder he observes or describes. He stops and chats with the reader, not in a traditional Texas "voice" but nearer that of a classics instructor, almost never failing to insert some tale or anecdote. Without Thoreau's political asides, Bedichek offers nature as the best solution to mankind's private despairs; old fashioned, but not outdated. Ironically, *Adventures with a Texas Naturalist* has outlived most of the books of Bedichek's mentors.

Adventures with a Texas Naturalist

ROY BEDICHEK

Illustrations by WARD LOCKWOOD
Foreword by H. MEWHINNEY

UNIVERSITY OF TEXAS PRESS AUSTIN

. . . And Other Dirty Stories

by Larry L. King

A number of Texans have left their home state, then after the passage of years, have either returned home or written, with a certain nostalgia, about it. Very few collections are as down-to-earth in tone and interpretation as . . . *And Other Dirty Stories.* Larry L. King's love of his Texas roots stands out. I think this collection of profiles and pieces remains the best writing he has done, even though he later wrote a number of plays (including the Broadway success, *The Best Little Whorehouse in Texas*) and very readable books.

. . . *And Other Dirty Stories* displays power and insight in such ruthless studies as "My Hero, LBJ," and there is the recollection of innocence and realism in his childhood remembrances, particularly "Requiem for a West Texas Town," which has become an obituary-classic, not only for King's tiny childhood town of Putnam (pop. 109) but also for all the Putnams across Texas that have been wiped out by such blind forces as Interstate Highways and shopping malls. King has written well, and stylishly, in other works, but this first collection stands strongest, particularly in its Texas portions, which comprise over half its contents. He catches the restlessness and frustration, and at the same time the love, that the state engenders. Although Larry and I were born within forty miles of each other—a short distance in West Texas—and probably saw each other in our youth, we didn't meet until 1966 when I wrote a not-too-kind review of his (to date) only novel, *The One-eyed Man*. King sent me a note, saying my review was fair and might prove valuable. He suggested we meet soon. We did, and I've had marvelous experiences in his company many times since.

... **AND OTHER DIRTY STORIES**

by Larry L. King

Foreword by Willie Morris

An (NAL) Book

The World Publishing Company
NEW YORK   CLEVELAND

Aransas

by Stephen Harrigan

This first novel by Steve Harrigan is an intensely emotional book which involves its setting (Port Aransas on the Texas Gulf Coast), the feelings of the society around Jeff (the first-person narrator), and the fascinating world of that near-human mammal, the porpoise. But it is more than a "boy and dolphin" type story. This is about finding your place in life in the place where life has put you. It also concerns the actions and ideals you may or may not adopt in the face of some severe and dangerous opposition.

But the value of *Aransas* is not just in its tender story of the fate of wild things. It is a readable and exciting tale of a boy and man in Texas doing an unusual job in an unusual place. It is a convincing story of the narrator's actions with his beloved porpoises that lead to his near disaster without accomplishing what he sets out to do. But the people in this novel, the Texas fishermen, the beach bums, even the villains (to the narrator's mind) are fully produced—not to mention the porpoises. What is the best action to take for the wild things you have captured and trained, when you see them taken over by by someone you consider unworthy? Sometimes, as the book develops, idealism is not the only answer, or even the best one. The foundation of *Aransas* is Texas and the people of that popular section of the Texas coast. It is heavy with place. All this is depicted with feeling, genuine love and emotion, and yet with a realistic view of Texas's natural world.

Stephen Harrigan has written well on many Texas topics and situations. Another of his novels, *Jacob's Well*, which includes a skin-diving project at that famous Texas landmark, has the same intensity and passion for nature as does *Aransas*.

ARANSAS

A Novel by
STEPHEN HARRIGAN

Alfred A. Knopf   New York   1980

Armadillo in the Grass

by Shelby Hearon

Shelby Hearon began her writing career almost as a hobby. Married to an Austin lawyer, she lacked some outlet for her lively creative sense, her need for self-expression. *Armadillo in the Grass,* her first novel, was the result of this seeking to expand her boundaries of self. The book was an immediate critical success, observed more, perhaps, by outside critics than by her fellow Texans. The personal results were even more important. She divorced her husband, father of her children, and began writing a series of acclaimed novels which probed not just the Texas social and cultural landscape, but delivered a witty but poignant message for independent spirits everywhere.

Although Shelby is not a native Texan and has lived in another section of the nation for several years, modern, suburban Texas has not had a better social expositor. And while she has written a continuing number of well received books, *Armadillo in the Grass* seems to me her personal best. I was living in Austin at the time the book came out, and since we shared publishers, I was given advance notice that a hitherto unknown writer was about to make a major contribution to Texas letters. Before long her name was one of those automatics arising when a list of best Texas writers is called for. *Armadillo in the Grass* catches a moment (of varying minutes, hours, or days) in the life of every woman when she has to ask herself how brave she may be—change or stay as she is? Clara Blue, long married, with children, finds unexpected artistry in herself and it becomes a challenge and a fear, because it clearly opens doors that require others to be closed. The book is subtle, gentle, but strong. No cattle queens, no oil-baron wives, no honky-tonk romances, but a story shaped by its Texas setting. And whether the author included parts of herself in Clara Blue or not, *Armadillo in the Grass* made her meet some of the same decisions that faced the artist in the book.

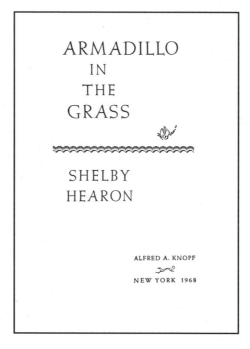

ARMADILLO
IN
THE
GRASS

SHELBY
HEARON

ALFRED A. KNOPF
NEW YORK 1968

Blessed McGill

by Edwin (Bud) Shrake

Unfortunately, *Blessed McGill* was initially overlooked by most literary critics, possibly because the author, Edwin (Bud) Shrake, was a sports writer, and it is an article of faith among professional critics that sports writers can't write about anything but sports. Bud Shrake has certainly written well about sports. In 1992 he edited and wrote *Harvey Penick's Little Red Book*, the best selling sports book in U.S. history that, with other books, manuals and training courses, has turned into a golf industry. The late Harvey Penick supplied the sometimes scanty notes, but Shrake did the writing, at the elderly Penick's request. But *Blessed McGill* has remained the author's favorite work, and in 1997 it was reprinted.

When I went to work for the *Dallas Times Herald* in 1960, Bud, Blackie Sherrod, and Gary Cartwright were on the sports staff, joined, or succeeded by Dan Jenkins and the late Steve Perkins: a Golden Age of Texas sportswriting. But all the time, Bud was writing novels which seemed to be reaching for some truth about Texas life that needed to be explained—books like *But Not for Love* and *Strange Peaches*. *Blessed McGill* combines the best of Shrake's talents: an acceptance of the absurdities of existence, recognition of irony's major role in the world, and a decent amount of historical and anthropological research so that the book never slews off into pseudo-historical "nonfiction."

Blessed McGill is subtly hilarious. It begins with an Austin boy, Peter Hermano McGill, after the Civil War, reared by a devout (but a little cuckoo) Catholic mother. By unusual circumstances, he becomes as much a brother to the Indians as to Anglo society. When McGill moves toward sainthood, it is not a mere absurd plot twist, but a study of what spiritual deliverance really is.

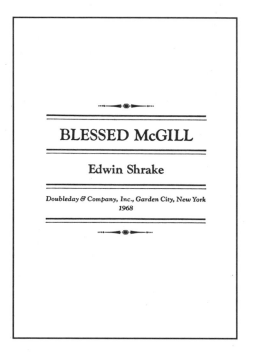

BLESSED McGILL

Edwin Shrake

Doubleday & Company, Inc., Garden City, New York
1968

Blood and Money

by Tommy Thompson

Although several good Texas true crime books have come out since *Blood and Money* appeared in 1976, they have lacked the dark attraction of this work. This book about Houston society murders and associated skullduggery is good literature, well documented—it has stood the test of legal challenges—and not one the reader puts down quickly or easily. Its importance does not rest on the series of crimes it may (or may not) depict; its choice for this volume is based on the late Tommy Thompson's skillful handling of a ticklish kind of story. And years later the questions of criminal intent have still not been answered, and the story will, perhaps, never have a true ending. But *Blood and Money* is a complete story; and sufficient in itself. In more recent years, writer David Lindsey has written a number of dark, criminal novels set in Houston which capture the sultry ambience of the true story and make excellent ancillary reading to *Blood and Money*.

(The first time I read *Blood and Money* I had a shock of recognition. I discovered I knew a figure in the tapestry of the story, and through her, had met one of the tragic major characters. Big as it is, Texas is still a small world.)

Blood and Money

THOMAS THOMPSON

Doubleday & Company, Inc.
GARDEN CITY, NEW YORK

The Bone Pickers

by Al Dewlen

Texas writers (as Larry McMurtry once charged) have paid
a great deal of attention to the frontier and the pioneers, but
significant works involving those second and third generations—the sons and daughters who didn't have to struggle
with nature and the elements—have been lacking. Al Dewlen
created a vibrant portrait of these cultural scavengers in *The
Bone Pickers*. When the buffalo were hunted off their Panhandle range, leaving mountains of bones for the settlers to
pick up, most families didn't brag about doing it the way the
old buffalo killers bragged about slaughtering the herds. *The
Bone Pickers* isn't a historical novel (unless the 1950s and 1960s
are already history), but it fits the historical metaphor, describing the slow dissolution of the Munger family of Ama-
rillo, wealthy beyond count from the ravaging of old crazy
Cecil, but shattered down to bone pickers by his descendents.
But don't let this brief interlude make you think this is another Faulknerian family dynasty novel. The Mungers are
Modern Universal, and sane—oh, except for June, who has
to have an ex-cop keeper. And the story of the family's de-
scent is a corporate one, mixed with political contrivance and
a touch of civil rights abuse. Jealousy, vanity, and the pres-
sures of money all figure in the lengthy saga. It's a Texas story
that could be laid in any part of the Lone Star State. When it
came out, Al Dewlen's novel had certain residents destroying

copies, I understand. Its burden has held up well, and a similar book could surely be written about a number of other Texas families and towns.

AL DEWLEN

THE BONE PICKERS /

McGRAW-HILL BOOK COMPANY, INC.

NEW YORK
TORONTO
LONDON

The Butterfield Overland Mail

by Waterman L. Ormsby,
edited by Lyle H. Wright and Josephine M. Bynum

By including *The Butterfield Overland Mail* in my listing of fifty-plus best books on Texas, I suppose I could be accused of a certain kind of partiality. I quoted it extensively in my own 1994 publication, *900 Miles on the Butterfield Trail.* But my naming *The Butterfield Overland Mail* in the fifty-plus list doesn't concern the Butterfield Overland Mail so much as it concerns Waterman Ormsby's writing about early-day West Texas. No other writer did better. The author was a young reporter for the New York *Herald* newspaper, hired to make the first westward trip on the Overland Mail stage from St. Louis, Missouri, to San Francisco in 1858. His first-person stories of that initial transcontinental trip showed that a good writer and a good reporter could, indeed, inhabit the same body. Ormsby noticed unusual and awkward things, yet wasn't sensational or judgmental—something uncommon even today in journalists traveling outside New York. He was witty, tolerant, and disposed to be amused rather than infuriated at some of the ridiculous events, places and people he encountered. Since much of the Butterfield route was across Texas, the state occupies a great chunk of Ormsby's delightful narrative.

In preparing to write *900 Miles on the Butterfield Trail,* my wife Judy and I followed the old route of the Butterfield Trail. We discovered Ormsby's dispatches to be as accurate and almost as usable as they had been when he wrote them, many portions of the remote trail having changed very little. (Although the title of my book is *900 Miles on the Butterfield Trail,* my wife and I actually traveled 1,900 miles, going from Oklahoma to California, but we liked the sound of the original mileage, 900 miles, suggested by the publisher, so we kept it as the title. The Butterfield Trail across Texas was approximately 900 miles.)

The
BUTTERFIELD
OVERLAND MAIL

By
WATERMAN L. ORMSBY
*Only Through Passenger on
the First Westbound Stage*

Edited By
LYLE H. WRIGHT AND JOSEPHINE M. BYNUM

THE HUNTINGTON LIBRARY
San Marino, California
1942

Charles Goodnight

by J. Evetts Haley

The late J. Evetts Haley wrote the Charles Goodnight story from first hand. It is as flamboyant, yet as down to earth, as its subject, but it isn't worshipful. Its glory is its readability. Haley wrote many other good books, but none touches *Charles Goodnight*. I hold it to be about the best Texas pioneer biography I've read, although on the whole, I've not cared much for writing that overly glorifies the pioneers, despite having been raised, in part, by an archetypal Texas frontier granny.

Charles Goodnight scrambled from orphan poverty to ultimately being the greatest (though never the richest) of the old time cattleman. (See Laura Wilson's *Watt Matthews of Lambshead* for a more contemporary cattleman.) Charles Goodnight had imagination, respect for ability, and sensitivity toward nature—but he was in a hardheaded business. Goodnight was a legend, but he wasn't a mythmaker. He came to Texas in 1846 at age ten and died in 1929, so his life spanned the history of the cowboy and ranching era on the open range. He fought Indians innumerable times, he scouted for the Texas Rangers, he helped open the Goodnight-Loving Trail to Colorado—but he also opened a college so the ranch families could be educated. He helped save the American buffalo from extinction, and he helped (reluctantly perhaps) bring civilization to the Texas Panhandle.

J. Evetts Haley was once outraged at a review I did of his 1964 political tirade, *A Texan Looks at Lyndon*. The review was picked up (without my knowledge) and distributed nation-wide by the Democratic National Committee, which helped cause sales to plummet. At a press conference Haley called me "a journalistic prostitute." I never could bring myself to get upset about it.

J. EVETTS HALEY

Charles Goodnight

COWMAN & PLAINSMAN

WITH ILLUSTRATIONS BY HAROLD BUGBEE

BOSTON · HOUGHTON MIFFLIN COMPANY · NEW YORK
The Riverside Press Cambridge
1936

The Comanche Barrier to South Plains Settlement

by Rupert Norval Richardson

The Comanche nation was, to the midwest—certainly to Texas—the most important and feared of all the tribes. The Comanches were not unusually fierce in the centuries when they inhabited the area around Montana, but sometime in the seventeenth century they found the horse, and a different tribe was born. More than any other tribe, they adjusted to this imported form of transportation, and they made it a weapon, a unit of commercial value, and even a symbol of romantic inclination: Comanche brides were purchased from their fathers by a gift of horses. Above all, however, the horse became the basis for Comanche warfare. The horse took them from their northern home, flooding down the midwest to Texas, New Mexico, and Kansas, pushing aside the other tribes and raiding and pillaging white settlements—anything for horses or, in some instances, slaves.

The Comanche Barrier was written well and professionally by a historian I consider the equal of any in the Southwest. It is not a history of the various Comanche tribal branches, but it makes enough investigation into the tribal past to satisfy questions as to how this tribe, never large in numbers, became the scourge and terror of the plains, even as they were being crushed to a remnant. The late Rupert Richardson's scholarship works the way a reader wants history to work: it fills in gaps, it informs when history is clouded, and it supports its contentions and conclusions. Only in the final paragraph does the author use a few romantic words: "They were finally defeated in the unequal conflict, but what a magnificent fight they made! (And) even yet, if we look by the light of an August moon across a Texas prairie . . . surely we shall see phantom warriors riding as of old—Comanches."

The Richardson Centennial edition of *The Comanche Barrier* was issued in 1991 by Hardin-Simmons University in honor of the man who spent his entire career at the school. It contains some 11,000 words which were edited out of the Arthur H. Clark edition for cost purposes. The 1991 edition was lavishly produced and, despite a steep price, quickly became a rarity. A softcover reprint also contains the added material.

The Comanche Barrier to South Plains Settlement

A century and a half of savage resistance
to the advancing white frontier

by
RUPERT NORVAL RICHARDSON
Professor of History, Simmons University

THE ARTHUR H. CLARK COMPANY
Glendale, California, U.S.A.
1933

Coronado's Children

by J. Frank Dobie

Frank Dobie's writings have, perhaps unjustifiably, lost a lot of their bibliophilic and critical glister since his death in 1964. Dobie, for one thing, wrote about an age and a culture (that indefinable word) that suddenly vanished from the forefront of Texas history and industry. Critics today (for what it's worth) pay scant attention to J. Frank Dobie except to shrug him off as part of the backward-looking generation of Texas writers, or sometimes praising him for his contribution to academic freedom, after his dismissal from the University of Texas.

But every Texas writer since 1931 owes Dobie a tremendous debt, for *Coronado's Children* is the book that first made it possible for a Texas writer to stay home and make a living. After *Coronado's Children* was published (originally by Southwest Press in Texas), it was picked up by the Literary Guild—first non-Eastern Seaboard publication ever chosen by the Guild or Book-of-the-Month Club—and became a national success. It has remained in print since first being published in 1930. The book created Frank Dobie's "Mr. Texas" image which, no matter how derided now, honored and motivated him for the rest of his life. The Guild payment was a pittance by today's standards, and his Texas publisher went bankrupt before paying Dobie full royalties; the consequences of *Coronado's Children* were more valuable than dollars. Dobie got a Guggenheim grant which enabled him to take off and do *Tongues of the Monte*, but more important, he could now sell anything about Texas he wanted to write; and this opened the field for those of us who followed.

Coronado's Children is folklore about lost mines and buried treasures, from which so many magazine writers have filched so much.

When I met Frank Dobie many years after first reading *Coronado's Children*, I told him it was still my favorite of his books. He acted hurt. I think friends convinced him his more serious works, like *The Longhorns* or *The Mustangs*, better fit his literary stature, for which he was quite concerned. When I was a Dobie-Paisano Fellow living on his ranch, his widow, Bertha, and I became friends, and I suspect she wished Frank had been more of a footnote-counter.

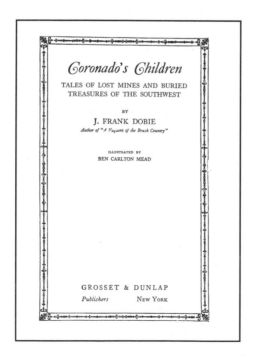

Coronado's Children

TALES OF LOST MINES AND BURIED
TREASURES OF THE SOUTHWEST

BY

J. FRANK DOBIE

Author of "A Vaquero of the Brush Country"

ILLUSTRATED BY
BEN CARLTON MEAD

GROSSET & DUNLAP
Publishers   NEW YORK

The Deer Pasture

by Rick Bass

Going to the deer lease to hunt each fall is a Texas ritual that has involved two, three, or even four, generations. Although deer hunting covers most of Texas, the Hill Country is the true center of the family deer lease, around cities like Llano, Fredericksburg and tiny places such as London and Willow City and Doss. Hunting deer, in some families, has become secondary to the gathering itself, a time of renewal and bonding with each other and the land. The Texas boy who is finally allowed to have his own gun and carry it on the hunt with the adults has truly made a Texas rite of passage. Rick Bass writes lovingly and understandably of all this in *The Deer Pasture*. This little book, his first, is not about hunting deer in Gillespie County; it is about living with a certain appreciation for life, and indirectly, Texas tradition. The country, the animals besides deer, the trees, rock ledges, canyons, streams, leaves and colors—the individuals and their attitudes—these are what really matter; these and the fathers, uncles and brothers who initiate or are initiated; the mothers, aunts, grandmothers who accompany the movement out to the lease, the daughters who sometimes join the actual hunt—they are what make these fall expeditions memorable, not just how many deer you shoot to make venison sausage. Rick Bass has written several major books and become a major contributor to American letters since the 1985 publication of *The Deer Pasture*, but none of his books has involved the Texas setting like this one does. (The illustrations are by Elizabeth Hughes, who later became Mrs. Rick Bass.)

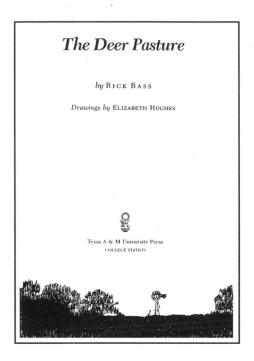

Ely: Too Black, Too White

by Ely Green,
edited by Elizabeth N. & Arthur Ben Chitty

Ely (EE-lee, as the English cathedral) Green was born of a seventeen-year-old black mother, Lena Green, born a slave, and a young white father in 1893 near Sewanee, Tennessee. Ely was taken in by a white family and became a sort of pet of some of the University of the South (Sewanee) faculty. At age four, Ely was baptized by the University chaplain, who later became Episcopal Bishop of South Carolina. But despite being able to pass as white—he did a few times in emergencies—he never denied he was black, or colored: he hated "negro," saying it was a slave word. Ely fled to Texas when he was nineteen, finding life too dangerous in Sewanee. In Texas Ely went to work for Judge Oscar Dunlap, a Waxahachie banker and a noble man who would not allow Ely to be persecuted as a black, even by the police—who tried many times. Judge Dunlap let Ely drive his car and Ely learned auto mechanics to become an expert. But even under protection of Judge Dunlap and the Dunlap family, he never escaped discrimination or deliberate persecution—and, to his own peril, he helped many black residents. Although *Ely: Too Black, Too White* is an autobiography (in Ely's unedited writing) and he moved to California many years before his death in 1968, the bulk of the book is Texas—all over Texas. (Ely drove for some of the biggest oilmen in West Texas.) It is a story like no other;

thrilling, tragic, but inspiring to white or black. Ely was a sergeant in World War I, was a champion boxer, and even after tasting the relative freedom of Chicago and New York, returned to Texas. One of the more poignant episodes involves his attempts to become an aviator. After Ely had repaired his Rolls-Royce, Colonel Vernon Castle (the famed dancer) told Ely to come to the Canadian airfield at Fort Worth and he would personally teach him to fly. Ely was driving to the field when the ambulance passed him carrying the body of Vernon Castle, killed only minutes before in a plane crash.

Page one of Ely Green's original manuscript

ELY

Too Black, Too White

by ELY GREEN

Edited by Elizabeth N. & Arthur Ben Chitty

The University of Massachusetts Press

Amherst 1970

26

The Evolution of a State

by Noah Smithwick

Recent critics of Noah Smithwick and *The Evolution of a State*, have declared certain details he mentions as faulty, but I consider some of the criticism to be nit-picking. *The Evolution of a State* is recollection, not history. It is not about heroes and heroic events. It is about everyday people in extraordinary times. There is not a more human document of early days in Texas—one that readers today can find themselves in—than *The Evolution of a State*. Smithwick, in his nineties and blind, had not lived in Texas for nearly forty years when he dictated his book to his daughter, Nanna Smithwick Donaldson. Some propose that the daughter composed the book, but any fair reader will consider this pointless, if nothing else. The book displays Smithwick's great human understanding, however much he actually penned. He was not well educated but he was broadly observant. Despite the fact that he makes certain errors, what he remembers is what most historians leave out: ordinary people, underlings, often as not.

He came to Texas in 1831, got banished for a while, then was back to see the Republic survive and become a state. Smithwick rose above the general pettiness of so many Texas colonists. He forgives easily, and what is more unusual, on more than one occasion he sides with the Indians and with "Negroes" who have been unjustly or prejudicially handled. He seems particularly fair about blacks, in a society whose leaders were seldom understanding—but he doesn't exhibit much sympathy for the Mexican foes. Smithwick shows a fine sense of ironic humor, particularly about himself. He is no respecter of persons; of sainted Colonel William Barrett Travis of Alamo memory, Smithwick opines, "he had not the qualities necessary to a commander." With the inevitability of Civil War, Smithwick, a Democrat but a Unionist, sold everything and fled to California. He never returned to Texas, dying in California in 1899 at age ninety-two. There are some who say he recites more than he knows. "Theories and conjectures are not evidence," he writes as if in rejoinder. If I could recommend only one book of early Texas, it would be *The Evolution of a State*.

Original Narratives of
Texas History and
Adventure

THE EVOLUTION OF
A STATE

By NOAH SMITHWICK

A FACSIMILE REPRODUCTION OF THE ORIGINAL

THE STECK COMPANY
AUSTIN, TEXAS
1935

From a Limestone Ledge

by John Graves

John Graves chose to leave the larger cities sometime in the 1960s to live on his acres of hard scrabble (as described in his 1974 book of that title), not as a country gentleman but as a working country man, raising livestock, growing various foods and fruits, and constructing his own habitation. Graves was not the first writer/philosopher to "go to ground," so to speak, but since the nineteenth century few have succeeded in producing as much amusing, thoughtful, and valuable writing from those self-isolated circumstances. In *From a Limestone Ledge* we find John Graves at his best as a personal essayist and an interpreter of rural Texas life. Most of these pieces originated as a series which appeared in *Texas Monthly* magazine, but Graves was wisely allowed to ruminate and speculate on life in a free manner. His topics are as varied as John's interests and expertness might dictate. But underneath all the wonderful forays into Texas life, man-made and natural, is an accepting mind, regretful of certain trends and changes, saddened by waste of the land or of lives on the land—but understanding and explaining the whys and why-nots of that land and those lives. "Blue and Some Other Dogs," one chapter of *From a Limestone Ledge*, has been made into a small book of its own.

John Graves

FROM A
LIMESTONE
LEDGE

*Some essays and other ruminations
about country life in Texas*

Illustrations by Glenn Wolff

ALFRED A. KNOPF   NEW YORK   1980

The Gay Place

by William Brammer

Published in 1961, *The Gay Place* has become the archetypical novel of Texas politics. Perhaps it will remain so, for it depicts an era which, in our lifetime at least, will not be repeated. The powerful presence on the national scene of such Texan giants as Lyndon B. Johnson, John Connally and Sam Rayburn dominated a long period when the Democratic Party held absolute control and Austin, the legislative and political heart of the state, was a place of back-room agreements and easily purchased votes. The vocation is politics, and the dominant figures are attractive but ruthless politicos.

Having stated all that, what can be said about *The Gay Place* as a work of fiction? It has been overpraised, it has been assigned values it doesn't possess, and some of this acclaim was motivated by sympathy for the late author. In the years since *The Gay Place* was published, the title has taken on a secondary meaning with which Brammer was unfamiliar, but the title comes from a poem quoted on the dedication page and is not about sexual choice. The time is the 1950s, but the date is unimportant; the book (actually three novellas) is still among our best reading concerning Texas.

I met Brammer at a publisher's introductory to *The Gay Place* in the old Baker Hotel, in his native Dallas. Billy Lee, as friends called him, worked as an assistant to Senator Johnson, and "the governor" in the book is assumed to be LBJ, although

Billy Lee didn't say so originally. *The Gay Place* is a fine but sad book, even if sometimes leaving the impression of a "work-in-progress," as if the writer had something more he wanted to say. But Brammer was superb at depicting the general decay of personalities and the sadness of the floating life. It should have made him a Texas F. Scott Fitzgerald. But Billy Lee couldn't conquer himself, and he never wrote another book.

William Brammer

The
Gay Place

being three related novels
The Flea Circus
Room Enough to Caper
Country Pleasures

Houghton Mifflin Company · Boston
The Riverside Press · Cambridge

Goodbye to a River

by John Graves

I am proud of the fact that in 1960 I was among the first Texas critics to announce the greatness of John Graves's writing. *Goodbye to a River* contains folklore, history, irony, classic references and dollops of natural philosophy, combining to work literary wonders. *Goodbye to a River* is the story of a man, in the 1950s, going down a river in a canoe and observing what is there, what has been there, and what it all can, and should, mean to other men. I have taught *Goodbye to a River* to creative writing classes as a metaphor (forgive me) for life: the narrator comes from the river trip a different man from the one who put in his canoe, and the same occurs to the reader. The river is the Brazos, and the sad prophecy of the title has, more than partially, been fulfilled. But the book goes far beyond the river and its history. It contains the basic humor, the rawness and old earthy wisdom—along with the hardheaded stubbornness—of a rural Texas society still to be found in certain not too remote crevices of the state. And this writing is done without sacrificing intelligence or historical accuracy, and yet with the acceptance of certain inevitable modern changes. Only a handful of American books have reached its masterly level. I still rank it the finest piece of Texas writing ever done.

(I have known only one reader who took strident exception to the theme of *Goodbye to a River*. She was in one of my classes at the University of North Texas, and she declared the book to be anti-feminist. "Everything except the river is *he*; Graves can't seem to accept the feminine." I attempted to defend the writer, pointing out that he not only had a strong and talented wife but was father of two equally talented daughters, to both of whom he was close and loving. The feminist critic, an excellent student, wasn't persuaded by these statistics. I sent John a copy of her well-stated argument. He wrote back, in typical Gravesian fashion, that he about halfway agreed with her.)

A NARRATIVE BY
JOHN GRAVES

Goodbye to a River

Illustrations by
RUSSELL WATERHOUSE

ALFRED · A · KNOPF · NEW YORK · 1961

The Great Plains

by Walter Prescott Webb

Although *The Great Frontier* is supposed to be his broadest contribution to history, and *The Texas Rangers* is more purely about Texas, my preference among Walter Prescott Webb's books is *The Great Plains.* Its scope reaches far beyond Texas—beyond the United States, for that matter—but it is Texas-inspired, and it explains more about Texan culture, even today, than just about anything written, or shown on television. Webb's idea of a unique plains civilization and its effect on history is a true contribution to social history without bogging a reader down in social science jargon (which is particularly deadly when mixed with history—as happens so often today). Sometimes *The Great Plains* even sings, something none of Webb's other books do unless an individual reader recognizes a challenging idea is being presented to him for the first time. But it is not a book one takes a taste of now and then. I think Webb wasn't taking himself so seriously as an international scholar when he wrote *The Great Plains*—a posture more evident in *The Great Frontier*, which can get downright unreadable. I must admit, some of my difficulties with Webb's writings may have a personal genesis. I found him almost unapproachable the few times I tried to converse with him. Those who know him better said this was the impression of many persons, but assured me it was wrong.

The Great Plains

BY

WALTER PRESCOTT WEBB

ASSOCIATE PROFESSOR OF HISTORY

THE UNIVERSITY OF TEXAS

GINN AND COMPANY

Great River, the two-volume set about the Rio Grande, is history to be read and absorbed. But don't let the length keep you from exploring the stories, for it can be read pages at a time as well as by chapters. When *Great River* first appeared, some writers charged it was as much fiction as history, lacking as it does the trappings of academic acceptance—overabundant footnotes and the citation of other opinions. Actually, critics didn't mean that it was untrue, but that it was written like a novel: the birth of a river, the sweep of the civilizations that lived along it—everything flowing along, a river of narrative as well as of water. It finds the romance of that essentially lonesomest river in North America: the Great River, Rio Bravo, Rio Grande del Norte . . . its names are interchangeable. There are passages within Paul Horgan's fiction that can't be surpassed for mood and sensual feeling, but most occur in his novels about New Mexico, not Texas. *Great River* is a Texas book, however, despite Horgan's preference for the Indian and Latin cultures of the river's upper course. The Texas portion, while the longest stretch, is a mere trickle in some spots. In 1993, while researching a book of my own, my wife and I stopped at the Rio Grande border crossing at Fort Hancock. With the border guard's permission, and while he talked with my wife, both being Missouri natives, I went to the center of the bridge, where the cast iron U.S.-Mexico border post is erected, and within the matter of a few minutes I made twenty-five visits to Mexico and returns to Texas.

G R E A T   R I V E R
T h e   R i o   G r a n d e

i n

North American

History

VOLUME ONE
Indians and Spain

by PAUL HORGAN

RINEHART & COMPANY, INC. *New York*
1954   *Toronto*

Hold Autumn in Your Hand

by George Sessions Perry

We Texans may have lost that direct tie with the earth our immediate forebears had: the importance of rain—too much or too little—and the roll call of seasonal activity; plowing, planting, tending, harvesting. But even in modern times, sitting in air conditioned ease or traveling the same way, we are affected by the land itself. Texas is primarily a place of lands, and different lands produce different peoples. *Hold Autumn in Your Hand* is a novel about a certain kind of Texas land and the men and women who did their best to live on it and make their living from it.

George Sessions Perry was a good writer, and his best works owe their power to the Texas society and its individuals they describe. *Walls Rise Up* is an amusing novel about two down and out Texans trying to survive in the Brazos River bottoms with as little work as possible, but I like *Hold Autumn in Your Hand* more. It goes deeply into the character and integrity of Sam Tucker, a tenant farmer in the Brazos bottoms, who, though poor, continues to fight nature, the seasons, the river, and more than a few of his fellow men, for the satisfaction of bringing something (including himself) from the earth. But the book is more than just another fight against nature. *Hold Autumn in Your Hand* is full of racy country humor and common sense. Modern readers will find changing times no barrier to the book's enjoyment.

In 1956 Perry's disabilities (crippling arthritis and alcoholism) led to his suicide when he deliberately walked into a Connecticut river. His frozen body was not found for two months. His suicide ended the most successful Texan writing career at the time. *Hold Autumn in Your Hand* was made into a film titled *The Southerner*, with Texan Zachary Scott playing Sam Tucker.

Hold Autumn
in Your Hand

BY GEORGE SESSIONS PERRY

The Viking Press · New York
1941

Horse Tradin'

by Ben K. Green

Ben Green began the best part of his writing career after he was in his fifties, and *Horse Tradin'*, the first collection of his tales (he wrote ten more), remains delightful reading, no matter that the period of the stories is remote—not so much in time as in our acquaintance with it. His narration is fresh and flowing, the work of a born storyteller. You never get tired of reading him. Angus Cameron, that noblest of all New York editors, then at Alfred A. Knopf, in 1965 asked if I were familiar with a Dr. Ben Green, D.V.M. I was the loser if I wasn't, he said, because Ben had written "Gray Mules" in *Southwest Review* and it was a classic (it is in *Horse Tradin'*.) I phoned Ben and started on a literary adventure not to be repeated; there can be only one Ben Green in a lifetime.

Ben worked by his own rules. One night he called and asked about a contract he had with "KAY-nop" (his version of the publisher's name). "I've got a contract for 85,000 words," he said. "Does that include the Introduction?" I said the exact figure didn't matter. "Th' hell it don't," Ben said. "I ain't givin' 'em nothin' they ain't paid for." He cut 640 excess words from the Introduction. Publication of *Horse Tradin'* made Ben Green a major writer, yet few of his fellow Texas writers would credit him. Why? Because he was also vain, dissembling, and impossibly cantankerous at times. For instance, those D.V.M. initials on *Horse Tradin'* never appeared on another Green book because they were false. He also tried to hide the fact he had been married and had served time in Huntsville. There are dozens of tales about Ben as colorful as the ones he wrote. Yet his writing in works like *The Shield Mares* proved his humanity was greater than he would admit. When the late Frank Tolbert and I attended Ben's funeral in Cumby, Texas, we noticed small surveyor's flags near his gravesite. We asked the undertaker about them and he said Ben had given several acres to the Cumby cemetery with the stipulation that if anyone were buried within fifty feet of him the land reverted to his heirs. "We sure weren't about to 'rouse Ben's ghost," the undertaker said, "so we sent a surveyor out here to make sure of the distance."

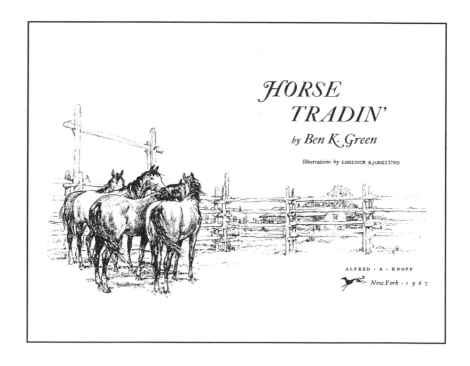

HORSE TRADIN'
by Ben K. Green

Illustrations by LORENCE BJORKLUND

ALFRED · A · KNOPF
New York · 1 9 6 7

Horseman, Pass By

by Larry McMurtry

Larry McMurtry protested that *Horseman, Pass By* was "juvenilia" when I included it in *50 Best Books on Texas,* and at a University of Texas literary gathering there were predictions of a grand feud but, alas for legend, we are still friends. McMurtry has written, or co-authored, twenty some-odd books to date, many made into movies (several receiving Academy Awards), but for me, this book remains among his best. I'm proud to have spotted *Horseman, Pass By* before most reviewers. I was book review editor of the old *Dallas Times Herald* when it came out and I was amused that the title of a West Texas book came from the great Irish poet, William Butler Yeats—in fact, from his tombstone. My brother David picked up the review copy and mentioned, "I knew this guy at North Texas State," so I read it and immediately caught the rhythm and truth in the writing. It is about a West Texas world I knew from carrying it under my fingernails, and every page struck a chime of recognition. In fact, Larry wrote me (before we met), commenting favorably on my review.

Horseman, Pass By views a changing scene and the people in it, contrasting heroic frontier virtue with down-to-earth modern effectiveness—mythology versus reality. The book speaks through the mind and eyes of Lonnie, a boy watching his West Texas ranch world sway and explode, along with his ideas of manhood. *Hud,* the movie made from the book, shifts emphasis from Lonnie to his arrogant, almost cruel—but ultimately the savior—uncle, Hud Bannon. It works well in the movie, but the book retains the art. While *Horseman, Pass By* won the Texas Institute of Letters fiction award (which dismayed some members) it wasn't a major sales success initially. However, first editions of the book now bring major prices, and it has been reprinted several times.

by Larry McMurtry

HORSEMAN,
PASS BY

Harper & Brothers *Publishers* New York

Hound-dog Man

by Fred Gipson

I was on the point of leaving *Hound-dog Man* off my list of 50+ Best, but I re-read it and re-discovered it contains insights into Texas culture that chronology has not obliterated. Some of the human relationships of the book (c.1905) are with us daily. Fred Gipson was a man who kept his private life pretty much to himself, but I suspect that Blackie Scantling, the hound-dog man, might well represent something of Gipson, particularly Blackie's views and attitudes about women—finally admitting (Blackie, that is) he needed something only a woman could give. (I once told Fred Gipson my suspicions about his feelings for Blackie, during a weekend retreat a few of us had. He laughed and said Blackie Scantling was a part of every Texas man. Fred died not long afterward.)

This was Fred Gipson's first book-length fiction and, as is usual with first books, it contains a crowd of stories—the veteran writer learns not to waste his plots all at once! The relationship between young Cotton and his idol, Blackie, becomes more than just the usual boy-into-man and man-tamed-by-love. It makes both developments reasonable and yet intriguing. It is not a juvenile in the manner of *Old Yeller*, Gipson's highly successful novel, but a more complex study of how a pair of males grow up, in their own ways. (I called *Hound-dog Man* "very near a Texas *Huckleberry Finn*" in the first edition of this volume.)

Gipson's paragraphs about nature are easily overlooked, but they are sensitive and sympathetic. He was an outdoor man by birth and nature. His passages about society and its components are even more evocative, and his handling of Blackie shows this artistry. Without Blackie, Cotton's story would become just a good juvenile book.

Hound-dog Man

BY
FRED GIPSON

Harper & Brothers Publishers
NEW YORK

The House of Breath

by William Goyen

The late William Goyen was a handsome and lovable man, looking the universal image of an author. Strangers who knew nothing of his writing fame seemed attracted to him. I ate with him and his wife in a Dallas restaurant (Mexican food; Goyen's choice) and people would come over and start chatting with him as if they were old friends. When his wife was along—Doris Roberts, the TV actress ("Little House on the Prairie" among other series)—it became hard to finish a meal. Children were crowded around her and the parents crowded around him. And despite the intricate, almost mystical, quality of his novels, leading one to expect an intricate man, difficult to reach, it was easy to know and make friends with him.

Although he lived most of his professional career away from Texas, his created literary world, Charity, was the setting for his best work. *The House of Breath* was his first novel and, in many ways, his best. East Texas has had a problem establishing a proper place for itself in national fiction. Neither southern nor western, before *The House of Breath* was published in 1949 East Texas was caught between folksy writers like Barry Benefield, of Jefferson (*The Chicken-Wagon Family*), the colorful Cajun culture nearby, and the Texas west. Goyen, in *The House of Breath*, created a region of memory that belongs purely to lower East Texas—the swamps and mists of the river area—and to some of its inhabitants. Goyen peopled Charity with characters such as Boy Ganchion, whose confession betrays the secrets of a dozen or so other characters in town. Boy Ganchion was tortured by the repression of his sexual urges, and *The House of Breath* created a stir among some Texas readers, for it deals with the idea in frank terms— although not with the four-letter overkill television has made us so inured to since. Charity is pictured in near mythical terms, its fate typical of the abandoned cultures of East Texas. Faulknerian overtones are present, but Goyen created his own East Texas landscape.

"What kin are we all to each other, anyway?"
AUNT MALLEY GANCHION

"JE est un autre." RIMBAUD

WILLIAM GOYEN   THE   HOUSE OF BREATH

RANDOM HOUSE • BOOKWORKS

I and Claudie

by Dillon Anderson

I and Claudie was first published in 1951, but its humor is reminiscent of the nineteenth century and O. Henry's *The Gentle Grafter*. Clint Hightower (the "I") and his sidekick Claudie are old fashioned con men who rather reluctantly have had to update their wickedness to take advantage of the modern, but more lucrative, field. They are capable (at least, Clint is) of doing business with one of Ben Green's mule traders, but their scam (a word not invented until 1963) is a bit more subtle—although not much. Now they are outsmarting bankers and oilmen, although about as often, falling victim to soft-heartedness or their own cleverness.

I and Claudie is a delightful book. One or two latter-day critics have termed it too ingenuous for our sophisticated age. Don't believe them. Clint Hightower would be right at home today in many an executive suite, with Claudie his not quite as dense, but not too bright, lieutenant waiting to take the fall for him.

I first met the characters of *I and Claudie* in a story in *Atlantic Monthly*. I wouldn't have thought to have ever seen Texas humor in such a Boston brahmin journal. Reading about the characters, and despite the elevated platform (and the old *Atlantic Monthly* was truly elevated), I was inspired to submit some humorous essays of my own. After the passage of time, two were accepted and both were reprinted in textbooks after they appeared. Alas, as I was getting on a first name basis with Charles W. Morton, the back-of-the-book editor, he died.

I later discovered Dillon Anderson was not some ink-stained wretch, but a highly successful Houston corporate lawyer. I eventually met him at a Texas Institute of Letters dinner, but it was one of those, "I really like your work" kind of meetings, and he died before I had the chance (or the nerve) to tell him how indebted I was to Claudie and Clint— and him.

I'll Die Before I'll Run
The Story of the Great Feuds of Texas
by C. L. Sonnichsen

The late Charles Leland Sonnichsen, Minnesota born, came to Texas to teach English literature, not to write history. Although he wrote much criticism (*From Hopalong to Hud* concerned film) and edited volumes of humor and folklore, he became better known for his historical writings. His most valuable Texas historical work is *I'll Die Before I'll Run,* and his histories of the El Paso area are quite good also. One of the advantages to Sonnichsen's history is that it is readable. Without taking sides in the inflammatory stories of feuds, he nevertheless holds the reader with the power of his presentation. As *I'll Die Before I'll Run* proves, fictional accounts of gunmen meeting for a showdown in the middle of the street can't compare to some of the actions— brave and cowardly alike—that took place among Texas feuds, covering the state from Teneha and Timpson deep in East Texas to El Paso and Laredo along the western border. Laredo was the only place in Texas (and maybe elsewhere) that a *cannon* was used in a feud. *I'll Die Before I'll Run* is well documented and as close to the truth as a writer can get when pinning down a feud. Attempting to document events of a feuding nature with court records is all but futile—even when the courthouse survives. (A suspiciously large number of Texas courthouses have burned.) Official records scarcely ever reflect what happened before and after the feud-inspired killings took place. Even today, a century or more after the fighting, some of the details can't be safely discussed in the old feuding grounds, no matter how trivial. In 1982, Sonnichsen told me he was still *persona non grata* in some places he would rather not name. *I'll Die Before I'll Run* has been much pilfered by magazine and adventure story writers, often without due credit.

I'LL DIE BEFORE
I'LL RUN

The Story of
the Great Feuds of Texas

by
C. L. SONNICHSEN

HARPER & BROTHERS PUBLISHERS
New York

The Inheritors

by Philip Atlee

Despite criticism that *The Inheritors* is "wooden" (as one critic put it), the novel's story is well told—thirty or forty years before its time. Few Texas books have been able to repeat the harsh dismay, the inspired brutality of *The Inheritors*. Some have resisted the idea that it might be one of the best books written about Texas, but if it is "wooden" it is also unusual: a Depression-era urban Texas novel—and most readers will find it good reading and thoroughly modern in its social interpretations. In the 1930s there weren't many novels of any kind being written about contemporary Texas, other than poor farmer or Depression tragedies. Edward Anderson wrote *Thieves Like Us*, based, in part, on the outlawry of Clyde Barrow and Bonnie Parker, but it was more rural than urban. What few Texans, and virtually none of its writers, realized was that by the mid-1930s Texas had become an urban state. The Texas Centennial Exposition in Dallas in 1936, for example, was the display of an urban, industrial state, sophisticated beyond the realizations of its own inhabitants. In *The Inheritors* Philip Atlee (James Phillips) wrote about Fort Worth—but not "cowtown." The characters are from the young social set—carousing, going from wild party to country club to all kinds of devilment, to eventual crackups, both physical and mental—an overindulged second and third generation, bored with the usual run of fornication, drunkenness and bragging about daddy's money. Not a few of the characters were said to be identifiable.

When I included this long-neglected work in my original listing of fifty best, the author wrote me an amused note, insisting, "Quit stomping on an old man's grave!"

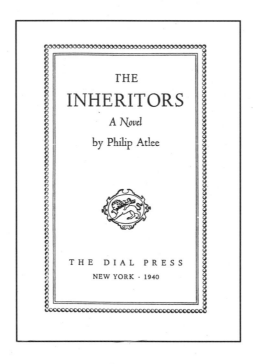

Interwoven

by Sallie Reynolds Matthews

The Anson Jones Press, of the late Herbert and Thelma Fletcher, published the first edition of *Interwoven* in 1936. The varied colors of the binding cloth prove it was done on a shoestring. But this was not meant to be a trade book. It was written by Sallie Reynolds Matthews as a memoir for reading by her children, grandchildren and a few friends. The rarity of that first edition has put its price beyond reach of most collectors. I own a copy of the Hertzog edition of 1958, the most beautiful specimen of his work: in typography, choice of artists, even a specially designed fabric for the binding with "M/ R" (for the Matthews and Reynolds families) interwoven— families whose affairs were (and are) so bound together as to be inseparable since frontier days, justifying the title. As for the book itself, when I taught courses in Southwestern and Texas writing at the University of Texas at Austin and the University of North Texas, I had a list of six titles I required everyone in the class to read. *Interwoven* was always one of the six. Invariably, students were delighted to discover it, and in the seven years I taught the course, I never had anyone disagree with this choice.

Several charming (but not always charmed) Texas women have written books about their experiences in early Texas: Mary Austin Holley, Jane Cazneau, Libby Custer, Melinda Rankin, to name some. But in *Interwoven*, Sallie Reynolds

Matthews gives us a lifetime view, not that of a visiting journalist or traveler. She wrote more about daily life on the cattle frontier than any comparable narrative. Sallie was bright, and even as a girl, she caught and understood the eternal rhythms of society which do not change. Born in West Texas in 1861, she tells of girls and boys in love, of weddings and babies and the bravery or foolishness of brothers and husbands—but never in a sentimental or worshipful way. She was very fair to the Indians, not characterizing them as savages. This is a delightful book. It is also a history of the women's part in the cattle business from the 1860s to relatively modern times.

INTERWOVEN
A Pioneer Chronicle

BY
SALLIE REYNOLDS MATTHEWS

★

THE ANSON JONES PRESS
HOUSTON   TEXAS
1936

Johnny Texas

by Carol Huff

Johnny Texas has been around a good while and has a couple of sequels, but the original book remains, in my view, the best of the lot. There hasn't been very much good Texas-based reading for juveniles. John Erickson's *Hank, the Cowdog* stories have become almost an industry in numbers, but the taped editions may be more attractive than the printed page for a youngster. Judy Alter's *Luke and the Van Zandt County War* is worthy of comparison with any Texas juvenile, but I feel *Johnny Texas* has a broader human scope and concerns a segment of Texas history that is as fresh today as when Johnny lived: a boy doing a man's job without complaint. Johnny is a German family offspring who works with a freight wagon to make enough money for his family to survive. But the book is not a harrowing tale of grimness. It is delightful—and even Frank Dobie, who didn't care much for juvenile works, said as much in his famous (but outdated) *Guide to Life and Literature of the Southwest.* History, Texas or elsewhere, is not a very prevalent topic for present day juvenile literature. More's the pity, considering the televised success of the Laura Ingalls Wilder books (*Little House on the Prairie*). Texas needs a strong juvenile that might make a television series as successful as *Lonesome Dove.* This might be possible with *Johnny Texas* and subsequent volumes. Instead, the nation has to accept the simplicity (or the unchallenging pap) of the A-B-C kind of child fare.

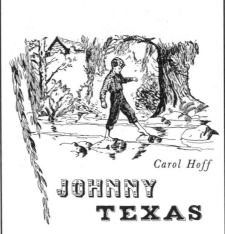

Carol Hoff

JOHNNY
TEXAS

BOB MEYERS ILLUSTRATIONS

Follett Publishing Company CHICAGO

Journal of the Secession Convention of Texas 1861

edited by Ernest W. Winkler

When *Journal of the Secession Convention* was included in the original edition of *50 Best Books on Texas,* a number of readers, going only by the fact the journal was compiled from state papers, asked, was this truly a book? I think the question answers itself with even the slightest dip into its pages. As I said before, this is the most tragic document in Texas history, and the most dramatic. Edited by Ernest W. Winkler, the State Librarian, the presentation is without comment and without any sign of persuasive attempts: the documents speak for themselves. Here we have the bravado, the unconsidered braggadocio and inflated egos of Texas leadership. Here we also have the quiet heroics of the scant handful of men who voted against secession from the United States, plus the public heroism of Sam Houston, Governor and Old Lion of the Republic, who resigned from his chair rather than see his beloved land rush into the inevitable doom the seceders faced. The lesser voices that clamored for his resignation give full cry to their own delusion and vanity. The *Journal of the Secession Convention* gives, without comment, the official votes, the names of delegates, the many motions and schemes that eventually led to the Lone Star State's participation in the greatest disaster in American history, from the convention's opening gavel to its final, self-congratulatory closing.

The publication of *Journal of the Secession Convention* was in 1912, and for decades—into the 1960s—available in a paperbound volume from the State Library, which sold for $2.50. Today it is scarce. It is the *Gone With the Wind* of Texas, dramatic and historic, but without any instance of happy heroics.

Texas Library and Historical Commission
THE STATE LIBRARY

JOURNAL OF THE SECESSION
CONVENTION OF TEXAS
1861

EDITED FROM THE ORIGINAL IN THE
DEPARTMENT OF STATE BY ERNEST
WILLIAM WINKLER, STATE LIBRARIAN

AUSTIN PRINTING COMPANY
1912

A Journey through Texas

by Frederick Law Olmsted

It is interesting to realize that Frederick Law Olmsted was more famous as a landscape architect than as a writer. He designed New York City's Central Park as well as famous parks in Brooklyn and on Staten Island. He designed the campus of the University of California at Berkeley, created Yosemite as a state reservation, redid the Boston Common into its modern form . . . the list is too long for this essay. Olmsted's *A Journey through Texas* was written as a result of a larger tour of the Southern slave states commissioned by *The New York Times*. The Texas journey was made after his travels in the South and the Texas book was published separately. In Texas, Olmsted visited Houston, San Antonio, Austin, Eagle Pass, and the German settlements (of which he greatly approved), as well as several coastal areas and plantations. (I wrote a small history of Austin in 1980, titling it *The Pleasantest Place*, quoting Olmsted.) *A Journey through Texas* is a very perceptive commentary on Texas society in the late 1850s (it was published in 1857). He was fair, and a professionally observant traveler, having visited in Asia and Europe. While he lamented the degraded condition of some Texans, he also found a higher level of civilization in the state than did any other Texas reporter. The book is both good reading and good sociology.

Olmsted didn't approve of slavery, but he does not let his disapproval taint his observations. As Professor Broadus

Mitchell stated, "Olmsted did what he could to save the pot [the slavery question] from boiling over. For passion he thought to substitute thoughtfulness; for raving, rationality, and for invective a calm examination of facts and their historical antecedents that should induce tolerance." *A Journey through Texas* has been reprinted many times and is still in print.

Lonesome Dove

by Larry McMurtry

Lonesome Dove is one book about which there is little question: it must be included in any modern list of best works about Texas. Despite having what some readers claim is a slow start, *Lonesome Dove* has immense holding power. McMurtry has skillfully mixed history, legend and his own fictional characters—and the book is jammed with characters, lovable or hateful, and on either side of the law. It is the ultimate trail-drive novel, with a subtle thrust now and then at our human frailties. It won the Pulitzer Prize for fiction in 1986, and the TV mini-series (scripted by Texan Bill Wittliff) was one of the most popular in TV history. The story is built around two retired Texas Rangers, Woodrow Call and Augustus McCrae. Gus is flamboyant where Call is cautious, conservative, and loyal in his love life. The two old comrades' decision to drive a herd of cattle to Montana is obviously motivated more by nostalgia than by any smidgin of common sense. Their crew scans the roster of the absurd—and some of the things that happen to the group stacks on more absurdity: rattlesnakes "balling" in a flooded river; a whore with a heart of gold that gets everybody, including herself, in trouble. Among the characters are a charming little girl who is a keen rock thrower, a rube deputy from Arkansas, a vicious Indian, and another Ranger, Jake Spoon, who travels a tragic path. There are so many stories going that McMurtry, now and then, simply pulls the plug on two or three. McMurtry saw the name *Lonesome Dove* on the side of a church bus and thought it was just right as the name of a desolate Texas border town—and a desolate soiled dove. Actually, Lonesome Dove is the name of a Baptist church near Grapevine, the oldest church (1846) in Tarrant County.

Lonesome Dove
a novel by

SIMON AND SCHUSTER   New York

Larry McMurtry

Love Is a Wild Assault

by Elithe Hamilton Kirkland

Texas writers have been fictionalizing people and events of Texas history since before the creation of the Republic of Texas, but Elithe Hamilton Kirkland's *Love Is a Wild Assault* does the best job of it to date. The book comes close to what has been termed "a bodice-ripper" of more recent years, but with colorful Robert Potter (first secretary of the Texas navy) and beautiful, much abused (by fate) Harriet Moore Page, how could it be otherwise? But Kirkland never strayed into the sensational for the sake of sensation. She didn't have to. *Love Is a Wild Assault* is about the romance and intimate relationship between the two historical characters and the thrilling but tragic development of their love—and Potter's treachery to Harriet. After tricking her into what he assured her was a marriage, on his death (by murder in the Moderator-Regulator War) he left the homestead on Caddo Lake to a woman in Austin of whom Harriet had never heard. Potter had come to Texas as an outcast from South Carolina, a hot-headed man with a streak of savage cruelty in him. Their home at Potter Point (still a landmark on gloomy Caddo Lake) was the scene of the final viciousness.

Love Is a Wild Assault is based on Texas history and on the autobiography of Harriet, who seems to have truly loved the rogue Potter. She tells of her attempts to prove their marriage bond was legal and to keep the home at Potter Point.

The book is passionately written because the true story was passionately lived.

Love is a Wild Assault
by Elithe Hamilton Kirkland

Doubleday & Company, Inc.
Garden City, New York

The Mexican Side of the Texan Revolution

by Carlos E. Castañeda

Carlos Castañeda, a native of Mexico, is not to be confused with the latter-day mystic of the same name whose works were popular in the seventies. Texas's Castañeda spent his educational career in the United States and his professional career as professor, librarian and Texas historian, at the University of Texas at Austin. The Perry-Castañeda Library there is named partly in his honor.

The Mexican Side of the Texan Revolution is not an attempt to explain or defend Mexico in the Texas Revolution. It is a documentary collection of articles, memoirs, reports, and records from the Mexican participants and Mexican government officials. The book is a necessary antidote to the hell-for-leather one-sided version of history Texans ordinarily get. Castañeda, whose loyalties were as much with Texas as with his native land, simply offers "the other side" and does a scholarly job.

From time to time a new Mexican literary artifact has been published concerning the battle at the Alamo, the Goliad Massacre or the battle of San Jacinto. Most of these Castañeda mentioned. However, the most important recent discovery was not published in English until 1975, several years after his death. This is *With Santa Anna in Texas,* the reminiscences (called a diary) of José Enrique de la Peña, a minor officer with Santa Anna during the Texas campaign. Peña gives a particularly acute description of the battle of the Alamo. After publication of this diary, the late Dan Kilgore upset the Texas historical establishment in his speech, "How Did Davy Die?" which suggested that Davy Crockett, instead of fighting gallantly to the death, surrendered and was immediately executed at Santa Anna's command. This version came from Peña (who thoroughly disapproved of many of Santa Anna's acts) and drew great attention to *With Santa Anna in Texas.* The book is immensely readable and forms a valuable addition to the Mexican literature. It has created controversy— one writer even calling it a mid-twentieth-century fake—and has appeared in more than one edition. The original Peña document contains anachronisms (it was written well after the revolution) and contradictions, according to its critics. But this doesn't decrease its value as another well stated and readable view of the conflict.

THE MEXICAN SIDE
OF THE
TEXAN REVOLUTION
[1836]

BY THE
CHIEF MEXICAN PARTICIPANTS

General Antonio Lopez de Santa-Anna
D. Ramon Martinez Caro (Secretary to Santa-Anna)
General Vicente Filisola
General José Urrea
General José María Tornel (Secretary of War)

TRANSLATED WITH NOTES
BY
CARLOS E. CASTAÑEDA
Latin-American Librarian, University of Texas

P. L. TURNER COMPANY
PUBLISHERS
DALLAS   TEXAS

Minding the Store

by Stanley Marcus

Sometimes it is hard to remember that an international figure like Stanley Marcus is both a native Texan and a lifelong
Texas resident. *Minding the Store*, his autobiography, gives a
valuable picture of growing up in a big Texas city—Dallas—
before World War I, as well as an insider's view of that fabled
institution, Neiman-Marcus. As Stanley (born 1905) puts it,
"As the store [which opened in 1907] was growing up, so was
I." He tells of attending public school where some classmates
yelled "Ikey!" and "Jewboy!" at him—Mama protested to the
principal and Stanley finally made friends with his tormen-
tors. But his Jewishness is a minor factor in the book. The
core is his major role in creating the store that brought more
fame to Dallas than any individual or activity. But this is a
candid recital, telling of young Stanley's often bitter work
under his father, Herbert Marcus, Sr., who forced his sons
into "minding the store" when some had as soon done otherwise. It relates the career—his own—that created that leg-
endary figure, the Rich Texas Oilman—or, more importantly,
the Rich Oilman's Wife. The book relates the internal
struggles between Herbert Sr.'s sister, the beautiful Carrie
Marcus Neiman, and her husband, Al Neiman, whose part in
creating Neiman-Marcus is often overlooked. Mr. Marcus's
children and his first wife, Billie, are also portrayed.

Minding the Store concludes five years after the 1968 sale of Neiman-Marcus—but the story of "Mr. Stanley" did not end there. He remarried and continued to lecture, produce (and sell!) books and write a popular newspaper column. In 1995 the Neiman Marcus company (the hyphen was eliminated) gave Mr. Stanley, on his ninetieth birthday, a magnificently lavish party which included "Cuvée Stanley" champagne.

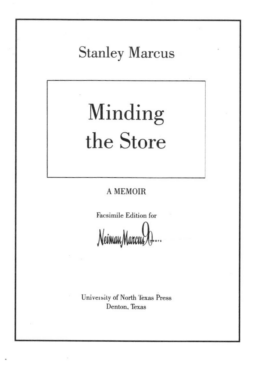

Stanley Marcus

Minding
the Store

A MEMOIR

Facsimile Edition for

Neiman Marcus...

University of North Texas Press
Denton, Texas

A Personal Country

by A. C. Greene

In the original Pressworks Publishing, Inc., edition of 50 Best
Books on Texas, *publisher Anne Dickson added the following
piece written by Bill Porterfield without A. C. Greene's knowledge. We agree with her and with Bill Porterfield that* A Personal Country *should be included as one of the* 50 Best Books
on Texas *and so are leaving it in* 50+ Best Books on Texas.
It qualifies.

This odyssey of West Texas is a classic and a worthy compan-
ion to John Graves's *Goodbye to a River*. If the list of best Texas
books were reduced to but ten, *A Personal Country* would still
make the cut. It is a good, a notable landmark for any writer
to leave, and it reads better today, years after it was first published, than it did when Greene finished the manuscript at
Paisano. Like jerky and whiskey and tobacco, it cures well,
and the older you get the more you appreciate it. It is the
voice that holds you. It is a perceptive voice, as intelligent as
the land it describes is broad, and it speaks with a flat, prairie
honesty that is profoundly American, out of the old rock.

Listen to Greene speak:

"I knew, for the first time, how much the place and the
past had created in my people what influenced me through
them. I thought of the size and shape of the experiences that
had made me and I wondered where and why it all began.

How much of me was red dirt, was sand hills and long, empty plains? What was born of slow-spoken closemindedness, gained from a frontier brush-arbor camp meeting, or what was begun in a dugout where a young girl looked in fright and hatred at the wilderness around her?

"And I began to see something beyond the land and beyond my blood with the land in it. . . ."

And so he takes us with him "on a billowy ocean of land" where there was "isolation in the grass and in the wind."

In *A Personal Country*, Greene works the same theme as Graves did in *River*. It is the conflict between inertia and movement. The movement seems a contradiction at first. To those of us who don't know it well, West Texas seems to be a bedrock of constancy, physically and metaphysically, even in a human sense. The fossils are not limited to geology. And yet fossils themselves are evidence of the cycle of life and death and rejuvenation. Nothing really remains put on Graves's river or in Greene's country, not even the dreams that would keep things as they used to be. The river changes and is changed. The winds blow, the grass surges and dies, the windmills whine and topple. Babies arc born and old folks die, towns crop up and decay away, the young people leave and the codgers hang on. It is all here, time, place, treasure, blood, sex, success, failure, death and, of course, god and the devil and grief, and the going on, as people must.

Bill Porterfield

A. C. Greene

A PERSONAL COUNTRY

ILLUSTRATED BY
ANCEL NUNN

Alfred A. Knopf / 1969

NEW YORK

A Ranchman's Recollections

by Frank S. Hastings

This is an unusual book about ranching and the cattle industry. Frank Hastings was not a cowboy and he did not inherit either the acreage needed for a Texas ranch or the cattle to stock the land. He was a ranch manager, hired for his business ability, not his association with the cattle trade. The cattle industry wasn't begun by the famous ranchers and trail bosses; the cattle *industry* was begun by the meat packers. They were the ones who created the market for those romantic Texas longhorn cattle. The trail led to Dodge and Abilene—but the packing house at the end of the railroad was the true goal of the trail drives.

Frank Hastings was university trained, coming to Texas in 1902 to run the Swenson SMS Ranches after becoming known over the world for his scientific knowledge of bloodlines in cattle. His work as a West Texas ranch manager (headquartered in Stamford) helped change western ranching from a gamble to a business; ranching is still full of gambles, but Hastings changed the odds a bit in the ranchers' favor.

A Ranchman's Recollections, fortunately for modern readers, is not a business book. It is charming and exciting, coming much closer to our day than to the days of the open range and trail drives. It is informal but informed; agreeable but accurate. It is good Texas history, as well as a memoir of an intelligent, adventurous man.

A RANCHMAN'S RECOLLECTIONS

An Autobiography

IN WHICH UNFAMILIAR FACTS BEARING UPON THE
ORIGIN OF THE CATTLE INDUSTRY IN THE
SOUTHWEST AND OF THE AMERICAN
PACKING BUSINESS ARE STATED,
and CHARACTERISTIC INCI-
DENTS RECORDED

BY

FRANK S. HASTINGS
Manager of the S. M. S. Ranch

STAMFORD, TEXAS

Published by
THE TEXAS STATE HISTORICAL ASSOCIATION
In Cooperation with the
CENTER FOR STUDIES IN TEXAS HISTORY
THE UNIVERSITY OF TEXAS AT AUSTIN

The Raven

by Marquis James

There have been many books, fiction as well as nonfiction, written about Sam Houston. They started coming even before his death in 1863. Many of these books are mere hack work, taking advantage of "I Am" Houston's immediate fame. (He was called "I Am" Houston because his sweeping signature made "Sam" appear to be an attempt to join the Biblical definition of God!) *The Raven,* published in 1929, remains the best biography of this great, complex, yet utterly human man who, much more than Stephen F. Austin, was the true "Father of Texas."

The Raven is melodramatic, of course. One cannot write about Sam Houston without melodrama. In a day when the average American man stood something like five-foot-six, Sam Houston was so above the average that he was seen as a giant—a melodramatic giant. (One biography of him is titled S*ix-Foot-Six,* although he was actually only six-foot-three.) *The Raven* might stand a little updating, especially in the unfortunate story of his first marriage, new facts having appeared, but it is still the best place to find Sam Houston. The late, great Texas historian, Llerena Friend, wrote a fine biographical book titled *Sam Houston, The Great Designer,* which emphasizes his political and diplomatic history, especially in relation to Texas. (There have been more sensational books involving Houston, but they are best left unmentioned.)

Marquis James was not a Texan. He was an Oklahoman, growing up in Enid, the major city of the 1889 Cherokee Strip Run, which he wrote about. When I attended Phillips University for a semester, my parents lived in Enid, and I shared their house. It was in the 600 block of East Oklahoma, said to be the oldest street in Enid, and local legend said the house had been Marquis James's home. I doubt the legend, but like the idea of having spent time where he lived.

SAM HOUSTON
A photograph by Frederick of New York City, made in 1856 when General Houston was a member of the United States Senate.
(Copy from the original plate, by courtesy of Major Ingham S. Roberts, of Houston)

THE RAVEN

A Biography of

SAM HOUSTON

by

MARQUIS JAMES

HALCYON HOUSE
Garden City, New York

Sam Bass

by Wayne Gard

Sam Bass was born in Indiana, it was his native home,
But at the age of seventeen, young Sam began to roam.
When first he came to Texas, a cowboy for to be,
A kinder hearted fellow you seldom ever see.

Sam Bass is still the most popular bandit in Texas history, probably because of the mournful ballad about him. Facts can never overtake legend, not in the case of an outlaw someone has written a song about—but the fact is, Sam wasn't a very successful bandit, and the melancholy of the song has elicited more sympathy than his short and bewildered life was endowed with. One cold January day on my way to Dallas, I stopped to see Sam's grave in Old Round Rock. (In a stream to the west of Interstate Highway 35, you can still see the big round rock for which both old and new towns are named.) As I was driving through the cemetery, I noticed a car that kept following me. When I got out to view Sam's actual grave, the car pulled behind mine and a man got out. He apologized, but explained that the tombstone on the grave of Sam Bass had to be protected. Through the years souvenir hunters had carried off several markers—in pieces.

Sam Bass, by the late Wayne Gard, doesn't fall into the folklore trap, although it relates some prevalent legends along with the facts. Wayne never forgets he is writing about a man, the facts of whose life are unimportant in comparison to what he is reputed to have done. *Sam Bass* is the most reliable account of the bandit, and Wayne Gard's best book. (Bryan Woolley has written a colorful novel about Sam Bass, sticking close to the facts without sacrificing the attraction of the legends.)

Sam Bass

By WAYNE GARD

WITH ILLUSTRATIONS

BOSTON AND NEW YORK
HOUGHTON MIFFLIN COMPANY
The Riverside Press Cambridge
1936

Sironia, Texas

by Madison Cooper

I've said it before, but am compelled to repeat myself: *Sironia, Texas* is a novel like no other Texas novel. It is colorful but mysterious, darkly hinting at, or frankly depicting, the activities of an early twentieth-century society which was more Southern than Southwestern. Waco, Madison Cooper's birthplace and home, is generally held to be the city of the title, and several characters in the book are said to have been taken from real lives. However, Cooper ordered his files destroyed, and the generation he wrote about (which was his own), has generally passed on. But this has nothing to do with the quality of the novel, and *Sironia, Texas* deserves more literary attention than the fact that, at 1,731 pages, in two volumes, it is thought to be the longest novel in book form ever published in the English language.

It seems to me that *Sironia, Texas,* if it is indeed Waco in disguise, could not have been written about another large Texas city. Dallas, in that same period (1900–1920) had nothing like the cohesiveness of Waco, and Houston, in this regard, was out of the question. San Antonio had a kind of closed society, but not comparable to Waco's close-knit cotton, mercantile and banking families. Madison Cooper, as owner of the Cooper Grocery Company, was quite wealthy, and on his unexpected death in 1956 (while jogging!) left his fortune to a foundation benefiting Waco. Was it payment of a debt? The

foundation has made hundreds of grants to local residents
and causes.

I owned a book store in Abilene when *Sironia, Texas* came
out in 1952 and I insisted that two literate, open-minded sisters buy the set. They did, but returned the volumes later, not
for a refund but merely to give me as a present. "I took a
bath, even washed my hair," one of the sisters said, "after I
finished reading it." That set is the one I used to write this
essay—and still have.

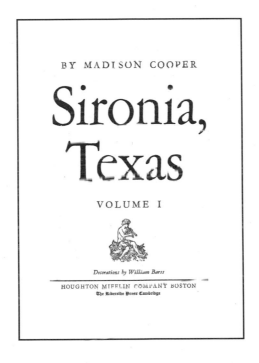

Six-Guns and Saddle Leather
A Bibliography of Books and Pamphlets on Western Outlaws and Gunmen

by Ramon Adams

Is there a need any longer for Texas literature to recognize the outlaws and gunmen who populate *Six-Guns and Saddle Leather*? I think there is, at least for another generation or two, at which time an updated compilation may be needed to include some of the bloody history of our later age. Six-guns may have become *passé* in favor of more sophisticated automatic weapons—and leather auto seats rather than saddle leather—but outlaws will continue, and will always have a following of readers who may not approve of the crimes, but thrill to the legends. In addition to its bibliographical value, *Six-Guns and Saddle Leather* is good and easy reading; more nearly literature than most such compilations. Ramon Adams, who came to Texas in order to play a violin in the silent movie days, did other books of lists: *Western Words, The Rampaging Herd* (which is about cattle books, and some may think should be listed here rather than *Six-Guns*), *Burs Under the Saddle* and *More Burs Under the Saddle*, the pair detailing some of the mistakes, errors and lies early writers indulged in. But I continue to use *Six-Guns* because it involves a more fascinating field, and is more readable in itself.

Ramon Adams was a strange sort of man who had facets of personality unlooked for in a historical and bibliographical assembler. After he hurt his hand and had to give up the violin, he became a professional candymaker. People who knew Ramon well enough to be invited to one of his Sunday afternoon "teas" can tell of some afternoons when Ramon would sit without saying a word for many minutes at a time, the guests obliged to do likewise. His talk, if it began again, was pleasant; he knew and loved the southwestern book world.

SIX-GUNS
& SADDLE
LEATHER

*A Bibliography of Books and Pamphlets
on Western Outlaws and Gunmen*

Compiled by RAMON F. ADAMS

UNIVERSITY OF OKLAHOMA PRESS
NORMAN

Six Years with the
Texas Rangers

by James B. Gillett

The Texas Rangers, like the Royal Canadian Mounted Police, may have outlived their days of popular legend, but their mark on popular history remains powerful. Movie and television viewers still respond to that powerful line of script that announced, "I'm a Texas Ranger." James B. Gillett's *Six Years with the Texas Rangers* is by far the best work ever done of that elite corps. He tells a straightforward story of working in the days when the Texas Rangers rode in companies, camped on the frontier, and in their own way, brought law and order to places where those principles were secondary to a great many people. The drama and color of the events Gillett writes about came from the events themselves, not from an over-heated pen. His regard for honesty is evident throughout the book. Walter Prescott Webb's book, *The Texas Rangers,* while held to be the basic history of the organization, is written with a touch of deification at which Gillett never hints. And he writes to be read; careful of facts but not academic.

I have found Gillett useful in writings of my own. He and Herman Lehman, the Texas boy of *The Last Captive* who lived with the Indians and became one, met in battle when Gillett, a boy himself (he joined the Texas Rangers at age eighteen) was tricked by Herman, who made an unbelievable escape from capture. Fifty years later the ex-Ranger and the ex-

Indian met, recognized they had been the players in the drama, and became friends. I used part of a Gillett chapter in *900 Miles on the Butterfield Trail.* I also included a true story, related by Gillett, involving a heroic dog among the ruins of an old Butterfield Overland Mail station at Salt Flat. Jim later owned a ranch near Fort Davis that included part of the Butterfield Trail. He raised a monument on his ranch to some of the old stage drivers.

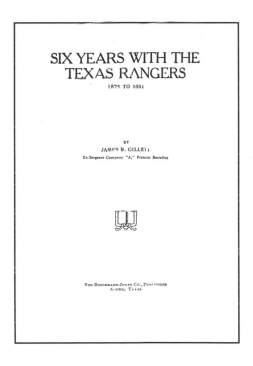

Southwest

by John Houghton Allen

In the decades since *Southwest* was published in 1952, nothing in Texas literature has been done to match this unusual book about an unusual time in an unusual place: the remote deserty back country of South Texas. And it was written by an unusual man. John Houghton Allen wrote from memory, for he had lived the privileged life *Southwest* is about. Allen is a poet, and these autobiographical essays (as good a phrase to use as any) are poetic—romantic in the better sense of the word. (I have a rare volume of John Houghton Allen's poetry, privately published.) He writes with understanding and sympathy for the *mexicanos* who have lived on the land since Spanish times, and the folklore that surrounds the land. But he also writes from the elevated stance of a medieval nobleman. His Randado (the Allen family ranch) is more like a mirage, shimmering on the horizon of history; a Brigadoon of a place. It seems right that today Randado is reported to be deserted and ghostly.

The author also describes an Anglo ranching life where the men are more interested in horses and hunting than they are wives, except, occasionally, for other men's wives. While the marital misadventures may or may not remain, the region still supports the remains of this isolated sort of kingdomism. *Southwest* baffles critics. It is quickly seen to be fine writing, but is it entirely nonfiction? John Houghton Allen left his Southwest many years ago, settled in Arizona, and wrote mainly for his own pleasure.

Southwest

by

JOHN HOUGHTON ALLEN

Illustrated by Paul Laune

J. B. LIPPINCOTT COMPANY
PHILADELPHIA AND NEW YORK

Texas in Poetry:
A 150-Year Anthology

edited by Billy Bob Hill

The value of this 1994 anthology, edited by Billy Bob Hill, is that it brings together a host of poems, some good, none really bad, and many fine, old and new, concerning themselves with Texas. Almost every poet of note who has done a decent poem on the state is included, and readers will discover (as I did in writing the Introduction to *Texas in Poetry*) that the Lone Star State has produced and continues to produce poetry of great penetration, poetry that defines or resists Texas attitudes; displaying personal hopes and fears; internal recollection that swiftly transcends geography to become universal—and does it as well or better than most Texas fiction. The old historic standards are included: "Lasca," "The Cowboys' Christmas Ball," "Cattle," "Planter's Charm" (somehow Clyde Walton Hill's "Little Towns of Texas" was left out), but the greatest value of this anthology is that it includes more than three dozen of the best poets writing today; poets like Walt McDonald, Naomi Nye, Lorenzo Thomas, Jack Myers, Robert Fink, Cynthia Macdonald, Chris Willerton, Betsy Colquitt, Carmen Tafolla, Tom Whitbread—and, of course, Vassar Miller. It includes much talent that is found mainly in chapbooks, or poets who continued to write, with not much statewide encouragement, over the past fifty years. As a reference book *Texas in Poetry* has a singular place among my chosen

50+, but as good reading, it opens a seldom explored country. (But I hope a future edition will include an index of first lines.)

Texas
in Poetry

A 150-Year Anthology

Edited by Billy Bob Hill

CTS/TSA
A Center for Texas Studies Book

This 1990 volume includes nine plays, the majority *by* Texans and all *about* Texas. Horton Foote's *The Trip to Bountiful* and Preston Jones's *Lu Ann Hampton Laverty Oberlander* are probably the best known, although most of these plays have had well received productions. R. G. Vliet's *The Regions of Noon* is the only previously unpublished work in the book. Besides the above, *Texas Plays* includes Ramsey Yelvington's verse-drama *A Cloud of Witnesses*, Oliver Hailey's *Who's Happy Now?*, Jack Heifner's *Patio/Porch*, Carlos Morton's *El Jardin*, Mary Rohde's *Ladybug, Ladybug, Fly Away Home* and James McClure's *Lone Star/Laundry and Bourbon*. While one or two may not be the best known work of the playwright, the published collection is a notable representation of Texas theater.

As important as the play-scripts are the biographical essays on the various playwrights by editor William Martin, with production histories of the plays. Also given are listings and dates for the playwrights' published works which, for some, include fiction and poetry. Together, these chapters form a reasonably full history of modern Texas playmaking. Omitted, for various reasons, are Tom Jones and Harvey Schmidt's *The Fantasticks* and Don Coburn's Pulitzer Prize winning *The Gin Game*, which have no Texas connection, and Larry L. King's *The Best Little Whorehouse in Texas*, a musical. Austin playwright Robert Schenkkan's Pulitzer Prize winning *The Ken-*

tucky Cycle was produced after *Texas Plays* was published. (See Preston Jones's *Texas Trilogy* in another chapter.)

Texas Plays

★ ★ ★ ★ ★ ★ ★ ★ ★ ★ ★ ★ ★ ★ ★ ★ ★

EDITED BY

WILLIAM B. MARTIN

SOUTHERN METHODIST

UNIVERSITY PRESS

DALLAS

A Texas Ranger and Frontiersman

The Days of Buck Barry in Texas
1845–1906

edited by James K. Greer

Not every reader will approve of *Buck Barry* (as the book is usually referred to). It has patches of political incorrectness, as we may see it, but not as Buck Barry saw it. He had little compassion for criminals (he hanged several horse thieves), he distrusted lawyers and, quite often, judges, and he hated cowards in any branch of the law. But *A Texas Ranger and Frontiersman* is an honest portrayal of people and places where outlaws and what we might call "white collar" criminals often tried to take over.

Buck Barry was elected sheriff, served as a Texas Ranger, and considered himself to be performing community service, even when such "service" involved vigilante actions. But the importance of the book is not in this phase of Buck Barry's career. He kept a diary during a period of Texas history that is otherwise little known or explored, and for which there are few reliable records. He was part of the Frontier Battalion which patrolled the Central and West Texas outlands during the Civil War. The battalion was, officially at least, a part of the Confederate army, but few of its men (including Barry) paid much attention to the designation. Its task was to protect the frontier from raiding Comanches and Kiowas, who realized how many men had left Texas to fight "over there." Barry tells of one incident I find nowhere else. Many union prisoners were brought to a frontier post to see if they could be fed on buffalo meat. "These were the only federal soldiers I ever saw," Buck adds.

James K. Greer was a genial man, and I was in the book business when his *Colonel Jack Hays* came out in 1952. I gave it the first autographing party. Sold six copies. I just didn't handle it right. But Dr. Greer (he was teaching history at Hardin-Simmons University) was convinced that Colonel Jack's story would be made into a television series—as, indeed, it should—and he told me of pacing outside a Los Angeles television studio, thinking about it—and what he was going to do with the money. The book was not on TV, but it's still in print.

A TEXAS RANGER
AND
FRONTIERSMAN

The Days of Buck Barry
in Texas

1845-1906

Edited by
JAMES K. GREER

THE SOUTHWEST PRESS
DALLAS, TEXAS
1932

A Texas Trilogy

by Preston Jones

There have been several well done theater pieces come out of Texas since *A Texas Trilogy* was begun in 1974, but none have found the same dramatic locale as Bradleyville, the site of the plays in the trilogy. They encompass a modern small town Texas that still persists, right along with most of the characters Preston Jones read so well. Preston Jones was a native of New Mexico, and only came to Texas to study at Baylor with Paul Baker. It is generally thought that, as a result of his having spent a summer working for the Texas Highway Department in the Colorado City area, that city became his Bradleyville. Perhaps. But Bradleyville can be located almost anywhere across the broad map of the Lone Star State. The trilogy (*LuAnn Hampton Haverty Oberlander, The Last Meeting of the Knights of the White Magnolia*—considered the best—and *The Oldest Living Graduate*) played to great success in Washington, D.C., but lasted only sixty-three performances on Broadway. The fact that the three plays were given on separate nights may have wearied the New York critics, even though there were several of us who sat through a straight presentation of the three one New Year's Eve at the Dallas Theater Center. Separate trilogy plays are still being performed.

Preston's unexpected death in 1979 undoubtedly ended a career headed toward more success. I was with him at the famous Dallas hangout for journalists, writers and players,

Joe Miller's, not many nights before he was hospitalized with stomach ulcers. Preston spent almost four hours outlining plays he planned to write and discoursing on creative topics in general—and having many drinks. He was so likable and unassuming that everybody wanted to buy Preston a drink. Liquor is hard on ulcers.

A Texas Trilogy

Preston Jones

The Last Meeting of the Knights of the White Magnolia

Lu Ann Hampton Laverty Oberlander

The Oldest Living Graduate

A Mermaid Dramabook
HILL AND WANG • NEW YORK
A division of Farrar, Straus and Giroux

13 Days to Glory
The Siege of the Alamo

by Lon Tinkle

In the years since *13 Days to Glory* was published in 1958, there have been other books on the siege and battle of the Alamo, some providing more information, and more speculation, than this one. Two or three such books even challenge, individually and collectively, the notion that the defenders were heroic or brave. Davy Crockett's death has been speculated on; did he die fighting or did he surrender and pretend he was a traveler caught in the fighting? But the legend and myth of the Alamo battle is what has kept it in the forefront of American heroics. Even the revisionists have not succeeded in destroying this status.

When Walter Lord's study of the battle, *A Time to Stand*, came out in 1961, I wrote a review stating that whereas Lord's work is more inclusive and historically evaluative than *13 Days to Glory*, I preferred the Tinkle book because it is more revealing of the minds and wills that were behind the fateful decision to stay on to death—the matrix of the myth. What kept those men at the Alamo to die, as Lord believes, somewhat needlessly. I got a phone call from Lon Tinkle the day my review ran expressing his gratitude, and wonder, that I made the statement. We were, at the time, book critics on competing Dallas newspapers. He had quivered (his word) all week that I might seize the opportunity "to elevate the fine Lord book and denounce that of your rival." (Those who recall the late Lon Tinkle's matchless diction can hear the inflections in that sentence.) I was the one to quiver when, a few weeks later, I introduced Walter Lord at a book and author luncheon; but he made only an amused reference to my review as we parted: "Oh . . . that."

13 Days to Glory gives the essence of the Alamo story without attempting to exhaust history's explanation. Tinkle does not hallow the slain Texans, neither does he insist all the legends are true. But the strange consensus of the defenders to stay and die, he expands—and that is what makes the book such uncommonly good reading. (When John Wayne's movie, *The Alamo* was made, Lon was paid $800 for the use of his title in the movie's theme song.)

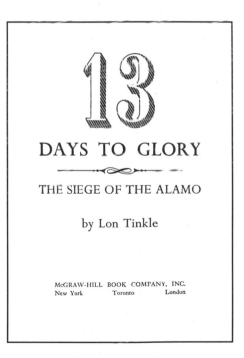

This Stubborn Soil

by William A. Owens

This Stubborn Soil is not the usual Texas success story. It is a story of determination to survive in a world that is suddenly, and fearsomely, changing. The twentieth century was eradicating old values and old traditions as swiftly as the calendar changed: week by week, not just month by month. As the title implies, it was a stubborn soil in which to grow. The fact that *This Stubborn Soil* is witty, rollicking, and full of appealing innocence places it in a secure literary niche.

To most Texans, pioneer biography was written (and lived) only in the nineteenth century. The late Bill Owens refuted that with his autobiographical series of which *This Stubborn Soil* is the first. This autobiography is about a rugged, still frontier-like life in the twentieth century, its opening chapters set in an isolated North Texas community with the quaint (but genuine) name of Pin Hook. It was still a frontier existence. The automobile wouldn't bring modern times to Pin Hook for another decade after Owens's birth. But the writer doesn't indulge in heroic cliché and claptrap about those backwoods people. He enjoyed boyhood, and writes about things like hymn singings and rhyming games, but he realized early on he had to escape—and his Pin Hook becomes a metaphor for all Texans (or Americans) who pull themselves away from their upbringing so as to transcend its more modest goals and social dogmas. Owens escaped to Dallas in 1923 at age eighteen, taking any job (or any break) he could get. But he was driven by a dream of college, though he left Pin Hook with less than eight grades of education. Bill Owens struggled and found what he sought: he became a respected professor at Columbia University. He wrote many books, fiction and nonfiction, most of them with a Texas setting. I think *This Stubborn Soil* is the best he wrote.

This Stubborn Soil

WILLIAM A. OWENS

Charles Scribner's Sons   New York

A Time and a Place

by William Humphrey

The late William Humphrey was a small man, not much given to gathering and talking about writing, or Texas, although his literary heart remained in the state of his birth even as he roamed the world. He hadn't lived in Clarksville for many years when he died, but his memory ran strongest there. In 1986, after much persuasion, Humphrey attended the Governor's Literary Conference at what was then called North Texas State University. He spoke quietly, if at all, and was something of a mystery man, even to some of his widely known peers. But after he had appeared on a morning panel, having little to say in the process, a busload of Clarksville citizens appeared—many of whom knew Humphrey as a boy and remembered him fondly, traveling quite a way to, as one woman put it, "visit a spell." The result was transforming, miraculous: William Humphrey became "Bill" or "Billy" and his whole personality changed. That upper northeast section of Texas, the setting for so many of his books and stories, was *his*, a place of home and heart. He made it into his country as surely as if he had been one of those hardy men who first forded or rafted the Red River to reach the Texas shore.

I find the finest manifestation of "Humphrey Country" in this collection of stories, *A Time and a Place*. Humphrey wrote other books about it and his life there as the son of a garage mechanic. He went back in time for *The Ordways* and used the deep Texas woods for his first, most successful book, *Home from the Hill*. (My favorite William Humphrey book is a slim volume, *The Spawning Run*, full of sly, elegant good humor about a fly-fishing time at a posh English club. He spent much of his writing career in Italy, England and Europe, or the East Coast.)

A Time and a Place is full of classic tales beginning sometime before 1920; mixing leftover community myth and mores of the nineteenth century with the often twisted interpretations of life peculiar to the region. What a shame that Texas has lost this adroit social commentator.

A TIME
AND
A PLACE

Stories by
William Humphrey

The Time It Never Rained

by Elmer Kelton

One spring afternoon in 1957 I was at home in dry, dry Abilene discussing her first manuscript with author Gwen Choate, and a heavy rain began to fall. When Gwen and I finally took notice, the street was running curb-to-curb in water. That was the end of the "hundred year" drought that had crippled Texas, particularly West Texas, from 1952 until that spring. That drought changed not only all forms of livestock business but also the social structures, particularly of the small towns. Despair moved in and thousands of residents gave up farming and ranching and moved into the larger cities. But despite pleas to accept "government money," and threats from financial figures, a few men like Charley Flagg, in *The Time It Never Rained*, stuck with it. Urged to sell out and give up, many did. Charley stubbornly hung on, refusing help and battling the bankers. In addition, his son and wife made life hell by rejecting ranching and sneering at small-town life.

Elmer Kelton has caught the tragedy and the stoicism that can make or break a man's (or a woman's) character, but understands that society changes just like business, and sometimes you have to change with it. When the drought ends, the West Texas world is never to be what it was before. Charley Flagg is a thoroughly sympathetic character who hates to give up, who tries to help the Mexican-American hands, who hates to sell off his sheep, and who almost kills himself under the pressure of nature's indifference: a Job of the prairies, who doesn't reap the material rewards of faith that the biblical Job received, but gains the greater rewards of human love. A realistic, readable story.

The Train to Estelline

by Jane Roberts Wood

In 1911, seventeen-year-old Lucinda Eliza Richards accepted a teaching job at White Star School on a Panhandle ranch near Estelline, Texas. She began writing lyrical letters home to her sister, her mother and friends back in old, established Bonham. At first everything goes so smoothly that young Lucy feels she has found her future: her classes go well, the family with which she lives is gracious, if troubled, and most of all (she tells her diary) she has fallen in love with Bob, the son of the big Sully Ranch. The romance begins with a sheltered girl, but while she is old-fashioned, her passions quickly mature with the man she loves. But this prairie idyll shifts to a more serious vein as Lucy makes increasing discoveries about what life can have in store: her dog, H.H., becomes rabid; Lucy wrecks her little Bush Runabout auto; her younger sister Katie, coming also to teach, is nothing like what Lucy had thought, and their sisterly relationship is estranged through an ultimate kind of reality.

This is an unusual novel about a time of alteration in Texas that is seldom depicted, especially with a young woman as protagonist. Lucy never becomes gushy or disdainful of the place or the people. The epistolary form works very well in *The Train to Estelline*, and those Lucy meets, from a young Mexican stray to the local fallen woman and her wild son, are well depicted. But the book revolves around Lucy and her

sister and the men who court the sisters, sending it to an unusual conclusion.

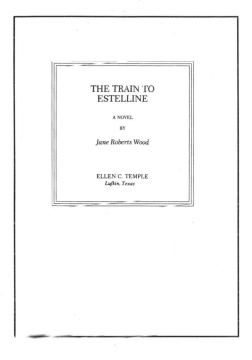

THE TRAIN TO
ESTELLINE

A NOVEL

BY

Jane Roberts Wood

ELLEN C. TEMPLE
Lufkin, Texas

The Uncovered Wagon

by Hart Stilwell

Hart Stilwell was a man with universal anger in his daily make-up. Sometimes it stood him well when he wrote, as it does with *The Uncovered Wagon*. In this book, written when Stilwell was forty-five years old, he finally and sardonically spills part of that anger on his father, called simply, "The Old Man" in the book. The book expands the miserable childhood of "Billy," a boy who is forced to travel the backroads of pre-World War I Texas with "The Old Man" in the title vehicle; getting whatever kind of field job, doing whatever kind of hard work. It is not a pleasant relationship, but makes an intensely readable book. Few readers will go through *The Uncovered Wagon* without some hint of recognition, either from personal experience or from personal observation. The Old Man is mean, unwilling to let Billy be a son, keeping him just outside the precincts of his heart. And Billy is not the only character in the novel who can't pass these chilly precincts: the world never gets much closer. It is a sad book, jarring at times, but written with balance between anger and compromise.

Hart Stilwell was hard to know, acting surly and (it seemed to me) unduly vain. He was a former newspaperman and wrote about it, but his major flow of writing was about the outdoors; hunting and fishing stories in all the major outdoor magazines. Once, at writer and newspaperman Bill Porterfield's

Dallas place, Stilwell was entertaining the group, singing and playing the guitar. He stopped suddenly and sat down, cross-legged and silent, on the floor. Bill, who had just acquired a twelve-string Gibson guitar, hesitated, then took it up and started strumming. I joined him on an amateurish harmonica. We sang through a couple of old gospel hymns and Stilwell loudly proclaimed, "That's enough of that (expletive excluded)." But Billy kept whipping his new Gibson, and I kept puffing away at my mouth organ. Hart Stilwell, without a word, began disrobing, and, completely naked, sat in the middle of the floor. When the music broke off, he started talking again where he had left off.

Uncovered Wagon

HART STILWELL

1947
DOUBLEDAY & CO., INC., GARDEN CITY, N.Y.

Watt Matthews of Lambshead

by Laura Wilson

When Watkins Reynolds Matthews died at age ninety-eight, he was the last living link with all the Texas cowboy and ranch mythology and lore from the 1850s, when his parents had moved to the edge of the West Texas frontier. But *Watt Matthews of Lambshead* is more than a book about one man on one ranch. Watt, as he was called, stood for something bigger, even, than his 50,000-acre Lambshead Ranch. He became American West history, and his ranch, his beloved community of Albany, his cowhands, horses, cattle, dogs, deer, buffalo—even coyotes, rattlesnakes and vultures—were the textbook from which he taught. Although he remained by birth (1899) a nineteenth-century man, he gracefully accommodated the twentieth century so that Lambshead was visited almost daily by neighboring ranchers, historians and artists of all kinds, and thousands of the famous or merely curious. Yet, in many ways, Watt anticipated ranching of the twenty-first century, and never settled for nostalgia.

Laura Cunningham Wilson, New England born but long-time Texas resident, was so inspired by Watt, Lambshead, West Texas and the communal joys of ranch life, that she produced, in sharp phrasing and inspired photography, a story that could as easily have been written in 1889 as 1989 when it was published. Here is the life of the working cowboy—a virtually eternal figure, working cattle amidst dust, heat and dangers;

cowboys on the open range and in the comradeship of the corral and bunkhouse. There is no flash or filigree to these men, just as there was none to their beloved boss, Watt Matthews.

WATT MATTHEWS *of* LAMBSHEAD

Photographs and text by Laura Wilson

Introduction by David McCullough

THE TEXAS STATE HISTORICAL ASSOCIATION, AUSTIN

A Woman of Independent Means

by Elizabeth Forsythe Hailey

This novel, stretching as it does from 1899 to 1968, is based on the letters of Elizabeth (Bess) Steed Garner, beginning when she was a little girl in the fourth grade. The story is carried by the letters of Bess, a striving middle-class Texas woman (in Dallas) throughout the first half of the twentieth century. Bess tells all (with the help of the author, of course) in her letters, and while she is strong and complex, she is not always admirable. She becomes an awful social climber after she becomes a wife (she married twice, neither husband meeting her expectations). Some of the most amusing letters involve Bess and her attempts to storm Dallas society. If achieving your goal is success, then she was successful. But as a wife and mother, she admittedly fails. One of the delightful things about this book is that the letters reveal so much more than the letter writer intended—and reading between the penned lines has a deadly fascination. (Part of the letters were actual missives from a female relative of Elizabeth Forsythe Hailey.) I read this story in manuscript, at the request of a friend, and saw at once it was classic in form and scope. I hope my enthusiasm helped inspire the author to continue in her sometimes discouraging attempts to find a publisher. The effort certainly repaid both Ms. Hailey and the publisher, for the story had fine sales and was adapted to a theatrical presentation. It also started Elizabeth Forsythe Hailey on a notable writing career.

ELIZABETH FORSYTHE HAILEY

A Woman of Independent Means

THE VIKING PRESS • NEW YORK

A Woman of the People

by Benjamin Capps

The woman of the title of *A Woman of the People* is known as Tehanita, or, "Little Texas Girl." Her name had originally been Helen Morrison before she was captured by the Comanches and became a Comanche warrior's wife and a Comanche mother. When Tehanita is retaken, years later, by frontier soldiers, she faces the impossible choice of leaving the people of her heart or going back to the people of her blood. The comparison of Helen Morrison to Cynthia Ann Parker is inevitable and valid. Cynthia Ann, too, was captured as a girl and later became a Comanche warrior's wife, and mother of the greatest Comanche war chief, Quanah Parker. But the stories are not parallel. Tehanita's story is a psychological study of what goes on in the mind of the woman, the counting and discounting of circumstances—and the absolutes of reality. Written in documentary style, *A Woman of the People* is fiction, but so convincing that one is tempted to pull down the *New Handbook of Texas* and see if maybe Helen Morrison (Tehanita) is listed. It is still Capps's finest book, although he has written a number of other good ones.

His first hardcover book was *The Trail to Ogallala* and it is a worthy addition to the short list of good trail drive works. I was book editor of the *Dallas Times Herald* at the time *The Trail to Ogallala* was published and Ben came to see me after my enthusiastic review appeared. Later, when I was a university professor, I used to group a number of trail drive books together for study and comparison: *We Pointed Them North* by "Teddy Blue" (E. C. Abbott), *Lonesome Dove* by Larry McMurtry, *North to Yesterday* by Robert Flynn, and *The Trail to Ogallala*. Every one of these books portrays a life that, at the end of the drive, becomes a different person—some disillusioned, some triumphant. The trail drive becomes a road of life.

Also by BENJAMIN CAPPS: *The Trail to Ogallala · Sam Chance*

A NOVEL BY
BENJAMIN CAPPS

A WOMAN

OF THE

DUELL, SLOAN AND PEARCE
NEW YORK

PEOPLE

The Wonderful Country

by Tom Lea

Tom Lea has the double talent of artist and writer, and one is unable to assign superior status to either talent. But as my immediate interest is in his books, his fine art work will be taken for granted. Lea's *The Brave Bulls* came out shortly after World War II and was a great publishing success, dealing with bullfighting better than anyone since Ernest Hemingway— or maybe even Papa. However, it is not a Texas based book. But *The Wonderful Country* is about a separate kingdom in Texas, the far western El Paso country that embraces a sort of lost literary land that includes parts of Chihuahua and Sonora in Mexico, and El Paso, his birthplace and the place where Tom Lea has lived and worked most of his long life. *The Wonderful Country* is superbly attached to the place—and the times and the cultures—of both sides of the Rio Grande. I have said before that this novel explains mysteries of motivation that history never delivers. The painter in Lea takes charge of the writer in almost every paragraph, describing clouds, shadows, sunlight and the rising and falling tides of sun- and moonlight. *The Wonderful Country* is set in a time, not quite antique but not quite modern; a condition this wonderful country preserved until very recently. The novel approaches the flawless, and the central character, Martin Brady (Martín Bredi), represents the strength of the region, and some of its flaws. One wonders, was Lea writing partially of himself?

BY TOM LEA
THE BRAVE BULLS
THE WONDERFUL COUNTRY

THE WONDERFUL COUNTRY

A NOVEL BY TOM LEA

WITH DRAWINGS BY THE AUTHOR

LITTLE, BROWN AND COMPANY
BOSTON

Index of authors, editors and titles